FAITH AND FASTBALLS: DEVOTIONS FROM THE DUGOUT

FAITH AND FASTBALLS: DEVOTIONS FROM THE DUGOUT

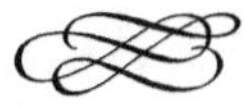

JUNIOR ARLBEE

This book is dedicated to God Almighty - my source of joy, strength and wisdom throughout this book. May the words on these pages bring glory to your Holy Name.

I dedicate this book to my three children - Isaac, Isaiah and Ruth. You continued to check my progress throughout this two and a half year journey as I wrote this devotional. Your thoughtful questions and suggestions inspired me to push forward, even when it felt like there was no end in sight! I love you with all my heart.

To Ruth, thank you for the cover design! Your creativity amazes me each and every day!

This book is also dedicated to all who read it. May your heart and mind be opened by the words found in this daily devotional. May these words encourage you on your faith journey and reignite the fire within you to pursue an intimate relationship with our Lord and Savior Jesus Christ.

And lastly, this book is dedicated to everyone who supported me on this endeavor. Your words of encouragement meant more than you will ever know. I couldn't have done it without you!

(Thank you for the office space!)

DAY 1

"The one constant throughout all the years, Ray, has been baseball…It reminds us of all that once was good and that could be again." Terrence Mann (James Earl Jones) Field of Dreams

Jesus Christ is the same yesterday, today and forever. Hebrews13:8

We live in a world filled with constant change. The weather, our feelings, other people's attitudes, our jobs. Everything is constantly changing. It seems as though nothing ever remains the same. And with change, often comes uncertainty. And fear of the unknown. But in a world full of change, there is one constant. Jesus Christ. The same Jesus who was crucified on the cross is the same Jesus we are called to pursue today. Jesus hasn't changed. He never will. His love for you remains the same. Yesterday. Today. Forever.

DAY 2

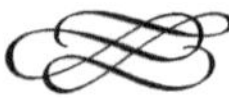

"Every strike brings me closer to the next home run." Babe Ruth

The godly may trip seven times, but they will get up again. But one disaster is enough to overthrow the wicked. Proverbs 24:16

We all fall short sometimes. Of our goals. Of other people's expectations of us. Of the glory of God. Failure is part of life. It's simply inevitable. No matter how hard you try, sometimes life doesn't go your way. But the question becomes, how will you respond? Will you allow it to overthrow you, defeat you and overtake you? Or will you learn and grow from it? Every failure can bring you one step closer to success, if you're willing to get up again. Ask God to help you grow from your mistakes. Ask Him to use your circumstances to mold you into the person He has called you to be. And for the discipline and strength to never repeat them. Amen.

DAY 3

"I see great things in baseball." Walt Whitman

Lord, there is no one like you! For you are great, and your name is full of power. Jeremiah 10:6

We use the word great to describe a lot of things in our society. We use it to describe how we're feeling, someone's athletic abilities, effort, talents. We use it in debates of who's the GOAT. But there is only one who embodies the true essence of greatness. And that is our Heavenly Father. He is sovereign. He is omniscient. He sees all and knows all. He is all powerful and He is worthy of our worship and praise. Spend today recognizing and honoring the greatness of God. Because just like the verse says, there is no one like Him!

DAY 4

"There's almost nothing worse than spending an entire day anticipating watching a Yankees vs. Red Sox game, only to have the score be 9-0 in the 3rd inning."

Tucker Elliot

I am counting on the Lord; yes, I am counting on him. I have put my hope in his word. Psalms 130:5

Sometimes life lets us down. People. Events. The weather. All things that are out of our control. But it's part of our human nature. We have expectations of how we think things should go. And when they don't, we feel let down and disappointed. But there's one who will never disappoint you, who will never let you down. And that is God. So today, instead of putting your hope in something that you have no control over, place your hope in the one who's in control. Count on Him. He will never let you down.

DAY 5

"It was one at bat in October of 1975 that defined Joe Morgan's place in baseball history and secured the legacy of the Big Red Machine, all with one swing."

Tucker Elliot

Let each generation tell its children of your mighty acts; let them proclaim your power. Psalms 145:4

So often, we feel that our life is defined by one singular event. And in a way, that's true. But more importantly, our life is defined by your response to that event. Because life happens. And sometimes it can be messy. But how you choose to respond to the events in your life will actually define your legacy. People are going to talk. They're going to tell others about what happened to you. That's out of your control. But your response can, and should be, a testimony to the mighty power of God. Because when you do, the story that's told, becomes His story, a story full of mighty and wonderful acts!

DAY 6

"Baseball is a good thing. Always was, always will be." Stephen King

Give thanks to the Lord, for he is good! His faithful love endures forever!

1 Chronicles 16:34

Stephen King could have substituted Our Lord for baseball in this quote and we would have had our scripture verse for the day! Baseball is good. But our Lord is better. God is indeed good. Always has been. Always will be. And because of His goodness, we should continually give thanks. The provider of all things good in our lives is The One who loves you unconditionally. Be aware of His goodness today as you go through your day.

DAY 7

"Baseball is a game with a lot of waiting in it; it is a game with increasingly heightened anticipation of increasingly limited action." John Irving

Rejoice in our confident hope. Be patient in trouble and keep on praying. Romans 12:12

Learning patience is difficult. We pray to God in our times of need and expect an answer immediately. And when He doesn't answer when we think He should, we get frustrated, doubting His love for us. In turn, we seek out quick fixes and solutions that often make our circumstances worse. But the Bible is full of believers who were forced to wait: Job, Abraham and Moses to name a few. Patience is part of growing our faith. Waiting. Trusting. Praying. It's part of the journey. God hasn't forgotten you. He's preparing you for a breakthrough! Just wait!

DAY 8

"On the baseball diamond, if nowhere else, America was truly a classless society. DiMaggio's grace embodied the democracy of our dreams." David Halberstam

Yet God, in his grace, freely makes us right in his sight. He did this through Christ Jesus when he freed us from the penalty for our sins. Romans 3:24

Grace changes everything. It's undeserved. And it can't be earned. But God loves us so much that He freely pours His grace upon us each and every day. Second chances. Redos. Mulligans. Every day we are recipients of God's grace. And His grace changes everything! Both in the here and now and eternally. Grace makes us right with God. So today, open your heart to receive God's grace and give Him thanks for it. And give others the same grace that God has so freely given you!

DAY 9

"Baseball really is a glorified game of throw and catch. And if you don't have guys who throw it really well, you can't compete for long." Tucker Elliot

Make it your goal to live a quiet life, minding your own business and working with your hands, just as we instructed you before. 1 Thessalonians 4:11

Throw and catch. Sounds simple enough. But anyone who has ever taught someone to throw and catch knows it's not that easy. It requires time, patience and repetition. And today's verse tells us to live quietly, work hard (with your hands) and mind your business. This also sounds simple enough as well. But it's not always as easy as it sounds. We live in a fast paced world full of gossip and distractions that values things, status and likes. And it's easy to get caught up in the race if we're not careful. But Paul instructs us to live simply. It's the life God has designed us for. So whether you have much or little, follow these instructions for a simple life. Live quietly. Live simply. And live for God. Starting today.

DAY 10

"Worrying about things you can't control in life is a waste of time both on the baseball field and in life." Tom Swyers

Can all your worries add a single moment to your life? Matthew 6:27

Bobby McFerrin once wrote a song called "Don't Worry, Be Happy." Only if it was really that easy! By nature, we are worriers. We worry about things that are out of our control and we worry about things that we are in charge of. But worrying is a waste of our time and energy. It changes nothing about the outcome and only stresses us out. Jesus's words are direct. Worry doesn't add any years or months or days to our lives. Birds don't worry about what they are going to eat, yet God feeds them. The lilies don't worry about what they're going to wear, yet God clothes them. And since you are more valuable to God than the birds and the flowers, be confident that God will provide for you. Starting today, quit worrying and start worshiping!

DAY 11

"It ain't over till it's over." Yogi Berra

Now all glory to God, who is able, through his mighty power at work within us, to accomplish infinitely more than we might ask or think. Ephesians 3:20

God's not finished with you. No matter where you are in life. No matter what you've done or accomplished. No matter how old or young you are. God is still working on you. You have so much more to accomplish for His Kingdom. So don't give up. Don't lose hope. God's best in you hasn't been seen yet. It's not over. God is just getting started! This is just the beginning....

DAY 12

"I'm not an athlete, I'm a baseball player." John Kruk

Dear friends, we are already God's children, but he has not yet shown us what we will be like when Christ appears. But we do know that we will be like him, for we will see him as he really is. 1 John 2:3

We all have different titles and positions in life. Son, daughter, brother, sister, father, mother, teacher, salesperson, athlete. The list is endless. But regardless of our title, we are all children of God. God created us in His image and likeness. We were created to be like Him. So no matter what you are, remember whose you are. You belong to God. You are His child. Don't allow your role(s) in life to become your identity. Because there's only one title that truly defines you!

DAY 13

"Every day is a new opportunity. You can build on yesterday's success or put it's failures behind and start over again. That's the way life is, with a new game every day, and that's the way life is." Bob Feller

Therefore, if anyone is in Christ, he is a new creation, the old has gone, the new has come! 2 Corinthians 5:17

New beginnings. A fresh start. We all need them from time to time. Build on our successes. Learn from our failures. But what if we treated each day as a new beginning and a fresh start? A chance to improve and grow closer to God. Scripture tells us that when we enter into relationship with Jesus Christ, the old has gone and we are indeed a new creation. A life in Christ is a new beginning. And each day is a new gift. So approach this day as a gift from God as well as the new beginning you've been waiting for!

DAY 14

"Do what you love and give it your very best. Whether it's baseball or business...If you don't love what you're doing and you can't give it your best, get out of it. Life is too short. You'll be an old man before you know it." Al Lopez

Work willingly at whatever you do, as though you were working for the Lord rather than for people. Colossians 3:23

It's hard to find motivation in life at times. Especially at work. Frustrating coworkers, long hours, too many deadlines. It makes you feel as though you're just going through the motions. No passion. No energy. No enthusiasm. But what if you took Paul's words to heart? And instead of working for your boss or customers, you committed your work to the Lord. Each day. No matter the circumstances. No matter the conditions. You work for God, not man. By doing so, you draw on the strength that God provides and you will find your joy in serving God!

DAY 15

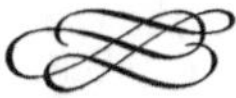

"People ask me what I do in the winter when there's no baseball. I'll tell you what I do. I stare out the window and wait for spring." Rogers Hornsby

The Lord is good to those who wait for him, to the soul who seeks him. Lamentations 3:25

Do you feel like your life is in a holding pattern? Or like God has pumped the brakes on your plans? If so, what are you doing during this waiting season of your life? Are you complaining and thinking about giving up? Throwing yourself daily pity parties? Or are you continuing to seek Him, no matter the circumstances? Because that's what God wants from us during these times! He wants us to grow closer to Him. To continue studying His Word and spending time with Him through prayer and meditation. Just because our plans aren't moving forward, it doesn't mean that the growth of our relationship with God should stop as well. God wants to hear from you. He wants to spend time with you. Seek Him daily, regardless of whether your plans are moving forward or not!

DAY 16

"I'd walk through hell in a gasoline suit to play baseball."
Pete Rose

Let your heart therefore be wholly devoted to the Lord our God, to walk in His statutes and to keep His commandments, as at this day. 1 Kings 8:61

Devotion. There are different levels of devotion. And we're all devoted to something. Our jobs. Our team. Our family. Our school work. What are you devoted to? Is it your faith? God? Because that's what He is seeking from you. Full, wholehearted devotion. Not a bandwagon believer. Not a Sunday/Wednesday relationship. God wants a 24/7/365 relationship with you. Starting today, devote yourself to God. Commit yourself to His Word. To prayer. To worship. And watch how your life changes, all because your devotion changed!

DAY 17

"Baseball has been very good to me." Roberto Clemente

The Lord is good to everyone. He showers compassion on all his creation. Psalms 145:9

It's easy to be good to people that are nice to you. That's pretty simple. But what about those that mistreat you? Or your enemies? That's a different story and a different challenge altogether. Because try as we may, it's difficult to be good to EVERYONE. But God, on the other hand, is good to everyone. Regardless of your background, history or poor choices. God loves us all and is compassionate to us all. His goodness doesn't depend on us. It's the essence of who He is. God is good. To everyone. So if the outpouring of your goodness towards others is subjective to their actions towards you, ask God to help you be more like Him. Starting today.

DAY 18

"There are three types of baseball players: those who make it happen, those who watch it happen and those who wonder what happened." Tommy Lasorda

You're the God who makes things happen; you showed everyone what you can do - you pulled your people out of the worst kind of trouble, rescued the children of Jacob and Joseph. Psalms 77:14-15 MSG

We serve a mighty God! He is a God who makes things happen. He leads us through the dark times in life and rescues His people who are in trouble. We see it throughout the Bible and in our own lives as well. Are you presently in a valley of life? Do you need God's mighty hand to rescue you? Call on Him! Ask Him to intercede. He is a God of miracles and wants to perform one in your life too! Ask Him!

DAY 19

"Baseball is the only field of endeavor where a man can succeed 3 out of 10 times and be considered a good performer." Ted Williams

We can rejoice, too, when we run into problems and trials, for we know that they help us develop endurance. And endurance develops strength of character, and character strengthens our confident hope of salvation.

Romans 5:3-4

Only in baseball does a 30% success rate guarantee you $25 million a year! We all face failure. No one is perfect and nothing is done perfectly every time. Things happen. Trials and problems are part of life. But when you face them, find comfort in knowing that you don't face them alone. God is always with you, holding your hand, guiding you through the troubles of life. And not only does He walk with you, God uses your trials to develop your character, strength and endurance. Challenges in life are opportunities for growth. Learn to view them that way. And the next time you face a trial in life, give God thanks. Because growth is about to happen!

trial in life, give God thanks. Because growth is about to happen!

DAY 20

"I really love the togetherness in baseball. That's a real true love." Billy Martin

Therefore encourage one another and build one another up, just as you are doing. 1 Thessalonians 5:11

Togetherness and fellowship. Both are important aspects of our faith walk. Surrounding ourselves with like-minded believers who love God. Who encourage each other. Who pray for one another. Have you surrounded yourself with other followers of Christ? If not, start today. Find a group of friends who value their relationship with God the same way you do. And pray for each other daily. Build one another up and support each other in difficult times. And in doing so, God's true love will be evident for all to see!

DAY 21

"Baseball is a lot like life. It's a day to day existence, full of ups and downs. You make the most of your opportunities in baseball as you do in life." Ernie Harwell

Live wisely among those who are not believers, and make the most of every opportunity. Let your conversation be gracious and attractive so that you will have the right response for everyone. Colossians 4:5-6

Every day you are presented with opportunities to advance the Kingdom of God. Through your actions and interactions with others, through your words and through your responses to adversity. And you must be prepared for each and every opportunity that comes your way. Even when things don't go your way, respond in kindness. When others are rude, respond gently. And when presented with an opportunity to share God's love, share it freely. Every day is a series of opportunities to further the Kingdom of God. Make the most of each one - starting today!

DAY 22

"There is no room in baseball for discrimination. It is our national pastime and a game for all." Lou Gehrig

There is no longer Jew or Gentile, slave or free, male and female. For you are all one in Christ Jesus. Galatians 3:28

"One in Christ Jesus." How comforting are these words? In a society that values individuality and a culture that looks to separate us by skin color and political views, let us be reminded that we are the body of Christ. We are all one in Christ Jesus. Discrimination and racism have no place in the Kingdom of God. Our Father in heaven sent His Son to die for the sins of everyone - not just the people who look like you, vote like you or speak like you. We are all brothers and sisters in Christ! And the blood of Jesus covers us all! As you go through today, treat everyone you meet like a brother or sister. Because that's exactly who they are!

DAY 23

"Baseball is a game of adversity. It's a game that is going to test you repeatedly. It's going to find your weaknesses and vulnerabilities and force you to adjust. That adversity…is a really good thing because it shows you where your weaknesses are. It gives you the opportunity to improve." Theo Epstein

We are pressed on every side by troubles, but we are not crushed. We are perplexed, but not driven to despair. We are hunted down, but never abandoned by God. We get knocked down, but we are not destroyed.

2 Corinthians 4:8-9

Life is hard. And sometimes it feels like we're being attacked from multiple angles. By multiple people. But Paul's words serve as a reminder, that no matter the adversity we're facing, no matter the confusion we're experiencing, God is always with us. He doesn't leave you. He won't abandon you. Instead God provides a way through the difficult times in life. He uses these times to teach you. And grow you. In doing so, it serves as a reminder of how mighty He truly is!

DAY 24

"If my uniform doesn't get dirty, I haven't done anything in the baseball game."

Rickey Henderson

But the words you speak come from the heart - that's what defiles you.

Matthew 15:18

Smeared eye black. Grass stains. Red clay from head to toe. There's nothing better than a dirty uniform after a hard played game. Sometimes impossible to get clean, they all make a uniform dirty. But Jesus's teachings remind us that it's not what we get on our uniform or even put in our mouth that defiles us or makes us dirty. Instead, it's what comes out of our mouth. Our words. Because our words are a representation of our heart. Tasteless jokes. Crude comments. They all come from an unclean heart. Is your heart clean? Does it reflect God's love with every word you speak? If so, keep it up! If not, ask God to clean your heart. And then let His love and mercy flow from your lips with every word you speak!

DAY 25

"In baseball, my theory is to strive for consistency, not to worry about the numbers. If you dwell on statistics, you get short sighted, if you aim for consistency, the numbers will be there at the end." Tom Seaver

So, my dear brothers and sisters, be strong and immovable. Always work enthusiastically for the Lord, for you know that nothing you do for the Lord is ever useless. 1 Corinthians 15:58

Aiming for consistency in baseball, or any sport, is a great approach. Consistent effort. Consistent results. But what about in other areas of our life, like our jobs? When striving for consistency can't help us overcome the boring, repetitive nature of the tasks in front of us. Those mundane assignments that seem to have no point. How do we approach those times? We listen to Paul's words. We work enthusiastically for the Lord. We commit ourselves, our time and our tasks to God. And that's where you find your motivation and enthusiasm! Because when you work for the Lord instead of man, your work takes on a new meaning!

DAY 26

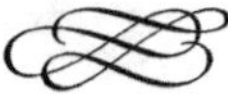

"Baseball is the only place in life where a sacrifice is really appreciated."

Author Unknown

There is no greater love than to lay down one's life for one's friends. John 15:13

The lost art of the sacrifice bunt. Intentionally giving yourself up to advance a runner and help the team score. It requires selflessness. A team first mentality. Putting others first. Sound familiar? Not only does Jesus teach the disciples what sacrifice looks like, he goes to the cross to show us what it looks like as well. Jesus willingly gave up his life so you could be made right with God. The Lamb of God was an example for us all. The ultimate sacrifice bunt. Jesus gave up his life for you; how will you repay him today?

DAY 27

"Trying to sneak a pitch past Hank Aaron is like trying to sneak a sunrise past a rooster." Joe Addock

Jesus replied, "I tell you the truth, Peter — this very night, before the rooster crows, you will deny three times that you even know me." Matthew 26:34

What's your relationship with Jesus like? Is it a relationship of convenience? Like when you need help or need something from Him? Or is it a relationship that you keep hidden? You don't want anyone to know about it and only interact with Him when no one's around? Or are you all in and fully committed? One of Jesus's greatest disciples, the one Jesus said He would build His church upon, denied knowing Him. Jesus predicted it would happen. But He forgave Peter and still loved Peter. And Jesus forgives us and loves us when our words and actions scream denial too. So today, instead of denying that you even know Jesus, tell everyone about Him!

DAY 28

"Things could be worse. Suppose your errors were counted and published every day, like those of baseball players." Author Unknown

And I will forgive their wickedness, and I will never again remember their sins. Jeremiah 31:34

Could you imagine if God recorded our sins and published them each day? Talk about humiliating! Psalms 130:3 poses the question, "who could stand if God counted all our sins?" But lucky for us, we serve a God of mercy and grace. And not only does He forgive our sins, He doesn't even remember them! He doesn't hold our sins against us. Instead, God chooses to use us in spite of our shortcomings. You have been chosen. You are forgiven! Thanks be to God!

<h1 style="text-align:center">DAY 29</h1>

"You may not think you're going to make it. You may want to quit. But if you keep your eye on the ball, you can accomplish anything." Hank Aaron

So let's not get tired of doing what is good. At just the right time we will reap a harvest of blessing if we don't give up. Galatians 6:9

Don't give up. Keep praying. Keep being kind. Keep allowing the light of Christ to shine through you. Sometimes we enter into difficult seasons in life and wonder if what we're doing is even worth it. If it matters at all. But it does matter. Because you matter. Paul instructs us to keep doing what is good. To stay focused on the Cross. To be devoted to your relationship with Jesus. And when the time is right, you will be blessed for your efforts. It may take longer than you thought, but whatever you do, don't give up. Keep doing what is good!

DAY 30

"That's the beautiful thing about baseball. You can be any size and be successful." Andrew Benintendi

For the Lord sees not as man sees: man looks on the outward appearance, but the Lord looks on the heart. 1 Samuel 16:7

It seems that we are naturally conditioned to look at outward appearance, height, build, beauty, etc. And depending on what we see, we form opinions on that person. Based on what we see, we judge and make assumptions about their character and their ability. But that's not what God sees. God looks at the heart. And He wants to know," Does it belong to me? Is my child devoted to me?" And when the answer is yes, He smiles. Because that's all God wants from us - our heart. Coaches and scouts are paid to judge players on size and perceived physical ability. And sometimes they're wrong. But God judges us by our heart, make sure yours belongs to Him!

DAY 31

"A life is not important except in the impact it has on other lives." Jackie Robinson

Share each other's burdens, and in this way obey the law of Christ. If you think you are too important to help someone, you are fooling yourself. You are not that important. Galatians 6:2-3

Jackie Robinson's life impacted countless other lives. For generations. Breaking major league baseball's color barrier in 1947, Robinson endured unimaginable racism and hatred. Yet in the midst of it all, he knew the importance of making a difference and impacting lives. And Paul did too. In his letter to the Galatians, Paul instructs fellow believers to "share each other's burdens." In other words, help them in their time of need. Don't think you are too important to help. Because we all need help from time to time. An encouraging word. A helping hand. A shoulder to cry on. That's how you make an impact. That's what's important. So make an impact today!

DAY 32

"You can't be afraid to make errors! You can't be afraid...
because no one can ever master the game of baseball or
conquer it." Lou Brock

Indeed, we all make many mistakes... James 3:2

Errors, both mental and physical, are part of baseball.
They happen. No matter how much we practice, no matter
how many reps we take, errors happen. And they happen in
life, too. But the fear of making a mistake should never keep
you from moving forward and setting goals. And living out
God's calling for our lives. Because our mistakes and mess-
ups do not define us. In fact, God often uses our mistakes to
teach and refine us. And in the aftermath of our mistakes, we
experience God's compassion, encouragement and comfort.
God knows you're going to mess up from time to time. But
He doesn't stop loving you. So keep loving yourself and keep
trying! Good things are awaiting.

DAY 33

"A winner is somebody who goes out there every day and exhausts himself trying to get something accomplished." Joe Torre

I have fought the good fight, I have finished the race, and I have remained faithful. 2 Timothy 4:7

Did you give yesterday everything you had to give? Did you "leave it all on the field?" Simply put, are you pleased with the effort you are giving today? Paul was. He saw his life drawing to a close and was evaluating his efforts and faithfulness to Jesus. In evaluating our efforts, we understand that we wear many hats in different roles throughout the day. We have different gifts, talents and callings. So the question you must ask yourself is, how are you using yours? Have you given it your all? Have you been faithful to God and the opportunities He gives you each and every day? If you haven't, it's not too late. Today is the best day to start!

DAY 34

"Never allow the circumstances of your life to become an excuse…I believe we have a personal obligation to make the most of the abilities we have." Jim Abbot

The man (Adam) replied, "It was the woman you gave me who gave me the fruit, and I ate it. Genesis 3:12

Reasons, justifications and self defenses. They're all excuses. And we all have them. Jim Abbot had every reason to make excuses. He was born without a right hand, yet still pitched in the major leagues for 11 years. He could have given up and offered up any number of justifiable excuses. But he didn't. When approached by God, Adam immediately shifted blame to Eve. Does this sound familiar? Is this something you do in your daily life? Instead of shifting blame or making excuses, own your mistakes. Accept your actions and newfound circumstances. And then make them better. Ask God for forgiveness and for help to grow and overcome. He's waiting to help .all you have to do is ask!

"I do what I've trained my whole life to do. I watch the ball. I keep my eye on the ball. I never stop watching. I watch as it sails past me and lands in the catcher's mitt, a perfect and glorious strike three." Barry Lyga

Humble yourselves, therefore, under God's mighty hand, that he may lift you up in due time. Cast all your anxiety on him because he cares for you.

1 Peter 5:6-7

Baseball is a humbling game. So is life, for that matter. Sometimes we get a little too full of ourselves, a little too proud. We start thinking that WE are the reason we are successful. That it's all our doing. When it's not. It's God and His goodness. Life can take you down a peg or two, just when you least expect it. Drops you to your knees. Which is exactly where God wants us to be! Calling on Him, sharing your worries and your concerns with Him. We are called to humble ourselves. And when we don't, life does it for us. So starting today, ask God to help you eliminate any foolish pride in your life and choose to walk humbly in His presence.

DAY 36

"Love is the most important thing in the world, but baseball is pretty good too."

Yogi Berra

And now these three remain: faith, hope and love. But the greatest of these is love. 1 Corinthians 13:13

Yogi nailed this one. Baseball is pretty good. But love is better. In fact, Paul refers to it as the greatest when listed along with faith and hope. But why did he refer to love as the greatest? Because love is an attribute of God! God doesn't need hope because He is in complete control. And He doesn't need faith because God doesn't have to believe in something else. But we do. And luckily for us, we don't have to choose which of the three we will live out. Because they all work together. Our hope and faith is rooted in love. God's love for us. So why is love the greatest? Because God is Love! Share it with someone today!

DAY 37

"Baseball is like church. Many attend, but few understand."
Leo Durocher

The beginning of wisdom is this: Get wisdom. Though it cost all you have, get understanding. Proverbs 4:7

Baseball is a game that for many people, is hard to understand. The strategies. The positions. The rules - both written and unwritten. It does get complicated. And many feel the same way about church. Stand, sit, stand, sit. Call and response. Do I need to say Amen now? What about now? What do I wear? But it doesn't have to be. And it shouldn't be. Church is about gathering with fellow believers and worshiping the One True God. And when you do, we grow in relationship with Him. We gain a deeper, more intimate understanding of who God is and who He created us to be. And that's the beginning of gaining wisdom. Knowing God. And knowing His will for our lives. Whether it's at church, at home or out in the community, seek wisdom. Today and every day.

DAY 38

"Yesterday's home runs don't win today's games." Babe Ruth

Not that I have already obtained this or am already perfect, but I press on to make it my own, because Christ Jesus has made me his own. Philippians 3:12

Living in the past. Whether you're reliving past mistakes or focused on past accomplishments, neither is good for your future. Learn from them. Grow from them. But press on. Keep moving forward. God doesn't want you to be content with what you've accomplished. He wants more for you and from you. More Christ-like. More service. More grace and mercy. More love. Paul spread the Gospel message throughout his life and as he was nearing the end of his life, he knew there was more work to do. He wasn't satisfied with the work he had done. And you shouldn't be either. God wants more. Of your time. Of your talents. Of your service. He wants more of you. Give it to Him. He is worthy!

DAY 39

"It's hard to beat a person who never gives up." Babe Ruth

This is my command - be strong and courageous! Do not be afraid or discouraged. For the Lord your God is with you wherever you go. Joshua 1:9

Giving up often feels like the only option. At the very least, it feels like the easiest option. But just because it seems like the easiest option, it doesn't make it the best option. Instead, when you are facing difficulties in life, heed today's scripture, "Be strong and courageous!" And find comfort in knowing that you aren't facing these challenges alone. God is with you. So giving up shouldn't be an option. Ask God to guide you and strengthen you. And watch what happens. When we quit, we accept defeat. When we call on God, we are victorious. Choose victory today!

DAY 40

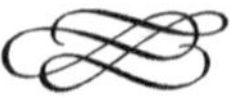

"I want people to expect more from me because I expect more. If you don't set goals high, you're not trying." Todd Helton

The lame man looked at them eagerly, expecting some money. But Peter said, "I don't have any silver or gold for you. But I'll give you what I have. In the name of Jesus Christ the Nazarene, get up and walk." Acts 3:5-6

Do you have a spirit of expectation? Do you expect to experience the goodness of God each and every day? If you don't, you should! The lame man expected a gift from the disciples. And He received one. And it was far better than the gift he was expecting. He regained his ability to walk. When we act in faith and expect God to bless us, He does. And oftentimes, it's so much more than we could ever have imagined. But it requires faith and a belief in God's goodness and provision. Placing an expectation on others often ends in disappointment. But God never disappoints. He will never let you down. God wants to share His abundant riches with you. Expect it and receive it. Amen!

DAY 41

"To succeed in baseball, as in life, you must make adjustments."

Ken Griffey, Jr.

Don't copy the behavior and customs of this world, but let God transform you into a new person by changing the way you think. Then you will learn to know God's will for you, which is good and pleasing and perfect. Romans 12:2

Baseball is indeed a game of adjustments. But so is life. In an ever changing world, we are required to be flexible and to adjust "on the fly." But one thing that should never change is our faith in God. Through commercials, family, peers and coworkers, we are often persuaded to change with the times. But don't be! Instead, remain steadfast in your pursuit of knowing, loving and serving God. Let God change you. The way you think, the way you act and the way you respond to adversity. And when you do, God will reveal His will for your life - today and every day!

DAY 42

"Everyone makes mistakes; that's why they put erasers on pencils."

Tommy Lasorda

For everyone has sinned; we all fall short of God's glorious standard.

Romans 3:23

We. All. Fall. Short. Each and every one of us. No one is perfect. No one is sinless. No one lives up to "God's glorious standard," no matter how hard we try. But luckily for us, God erased our sins through the sacrifice of His Son Jesus Christ before we were even born! Talk about love! But even though we know God will forgive us, it doesn't give you a free pass to say and do whatever you want. Strive each day to live up to His standard. Even if it's unattainable, even if you continuously fall short, let it be your goal for today. It's the least you can do!

DAY 43

"My motto was always to keep swinging." Hank Aaron

But as for you, be strong and courageous, for your work will be rewarded.

2 Chronicles 15:7

The circumstances in our lives can be frustrating. And sometimes, the outcomes of those circumstances can be even more frustrating. To the point of wanting to give up. To quit trying. But don't. Keep swinging. Because God sees your effort. He sees your work. Don't get discouraged by the outcome. Find happiness and joy in your pursuit of loving, serving and knowing God. And be patient. Your reward is on the way!

DAY 44

"Never give up. Don't cave." Jim "The Rookie" Morris

Blessed is the man who remains steadfast under trial, for when he has stood the test he will receive the crown of life, which God has promised to those who love him. James 1:12

Nowhere in the Bible does it say, "Those who love Jesus will never suffer or face challenges in life." Trials are part of life. Even for Christians. Especially for Christians. But the key to overcoming our trials in life is remaining steadfast. Steadfast in prayer. Steadfast in worship. Steadfast in hope. God accompanies us throughout life on our journey. Through the good times. And the not so good times. He promises that He will always be with us. But it's up to you to never give up and keep moving forward. And when you do, and your trial is in the past, you will be rewarded in ways you never could have imagined. Commit to never caving! No matter your circumstances!

DAY 45

"Set your goals high and don't stop until you get there." Bo Jackson

You need to persevere so that when you have done the will of God, you will receive what he has promised. Hebrews 10:36

Do you set goals for yourself? Daily goals? Weekly goals? Lifetime goals? If so, you know firsthand the frustrations and challenges that often come with achieving those goals. It's never easy. But it's always worth it. Especially when those goals align with the call God has placed on your life. Achieving goals requires perseverance and determination. And lots of prayers. When you rely on God to help you attain your goals, the journey often becomes more important than the destination. Your journey will develop discipline, devotion and character. And God uses your journey to refine you and grow you. And reach your full potential. So what is your goal for today? Being more like Christ is a good one to start with!

DAY 46

"Work hard and have patience." Randy Johnson

Whoever is patient has great understanding, but one who is quick tempered displays folly. Proverbs 14:29

We are not born patient. It is not something that comes naturally. And unfortunately, the only way to develop patience is to be put in situations where we learn how to be patient. Through waiting and delays. It's never easy and it's rarely fun. We want instant results and instant gratification. Especially after we've put in time and hard work. We want to see the fruits of our labor immediately. Learning patience allows you to wait joyfully, eagerly anticipating the outcome. When we ask God to grant us patience, he doesn't just give it to you. He gives you chances to develop it. So recognize these opportunities as gifts from God. He is patient and understanding with you. And He wants you to be patient and understanding with others. Lucky for us, God patiently teaches how to be patient, thanks be to God!

DAY 47

"So say, Hey Willie, tell Ty Cobb and Joe DiMaggio, don't say it ain't so, you know the time is now." John Fogerty (Centerfield)

This is all the more urgent, for you know how late it is; time is running out. Wake up, for our salvation is nearer than when we first believed. Romans 13:11

Have you accepted Jesus as Lord of your life? Have you accepted the gift of eternal salvation? If the answer is no or not yet, the time is now! Time is indeed running out. None of us are promised tomorrow. None of us know what tomorrow will bring. So accept Him and His gift of salvation. Today. And if you have accepted God's gift of salvation, continue to grow daily in His Word and allow Him to work in you - and through you, knowing that your words, actions and examples may lead to a life-changing decision for someone else. The world needs you. Now!

DAY 48

"It never ceases to amaze me how many of baseball's wounds are self-inflicted."

Bill Veeck

Remember, it is sin to know what you ought to do and then not do it.

James 4:17

Doing the right thing is not always the easiest path in life. Even when we know it's the right path. Doing good is often met with resistance and ridicule from others, which makes our decision to do the right thing all the more difficult. So we are tempted to follow the crowd, follow our peers and follow the world and the path of least resistance. But we are reminded in today's scripture that knowing the right choice and not following through is a sin. Especially when it comes to keeping the commandments, following the teachings of Christ and living out God's will for your life. When you intentionally stray from God's Word, you are inflicting self harm. And unfortunately, those choices often affect others as well. Today, ask God to help you make the right choices, to forgive your poor choices and to guide you in all your decision making.

DAY 49

"I have a good feeling about this club. But that could be gas."
Mike Hargrove

I pray that God, the source of hope, will fill you completely with joy and peace because you trust in him. Then you will overflow with confident hope through the power of the Holy Spirit. Romans 15:13

Are you approaching this day with a good feeling? With hope? If you aren't, you should! And here's why...we serve a God of hope! And God wants us to be full of His hope. When we are filled with hope through the Holy Spirit, joy and peace quickly follow. As believers, we know that God can accomplish anything for us, through us and in us. And that is what gives us hope. When your heart is filled with hope, you can find peace and joy in any situation you find yourself in. Knowing that God is with you, working your situations out for His heavenly purpose. So today and every day, be filled with hope! And trust God completely, no matter what you are facing!

DAY 50

"The designated hitter rule is like letting someone else take Wilt Chamberlain's free throws." Rick Wise

But get up and stand on your feet, for I have appeared to you for this reason, to designate you in advance as a servant and witness to the things you have seen and to the things in which I will appear to you. Acts 26:16

Wouldn't it be nice if we could have a designated helper for the things we aren't very good at or don't like doing? Kinda like pitchers do in baseball? Maybe it's doing the laundry or washing dishes? Or conducting meetings or compiling reports for presentations? Or anything challenging or hard? Jesus designated Paul (formerly Saul) to be his servant and tell others about his experience and about Jesus to the Gentiles. This designation and assignment eventually led to Paul's imprisonment, his shipwreck and ultimately his death. By no means was this an easy assignment. But Jesus vowed to be with him, leading the way and giving him the words to write and say. And Jesus does the same thing for you! No matter the task, the level of difficulty or the amount of resistance you face, Jesus is always with you, leading the way. You have been designated for the assignment of this day! Accept it with joy and ask God to show you the way!

DAY 51

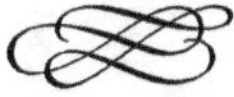

"A full mind is an empty bat." Branch Rickey

The Lord will fight for you; you only need to be still. Exodus 14:14

Overthinking. We all do it. Taking a perfectly normal, approachable situation and thinking of all the "what if's" and all the things that could go wrong. Before we know it, we're paralyzed with fear and anxiety. And our response often becomes an attempt to control our situation, the circumstances and the outcome. But God promises to fight for you in these situations. We just have to be still and listen to Him. And when you do, you will find that God can and will perform amazing miracles!

DAY 52

"One of the beautiful things about baseball is that every once in a while, you come into a situation where you want to and where you have to, reach down and prove something." Nolan Ryan

Obviously, I'm not trying to win the approval of people, but of God. If pleasing people were my goal, I would not be Christ's servant. Galatians 1:10

Are your plans for today to please others with your words and actions or to please God? Hopefully it's to please God. Paul faced this dilemma almost everywhere he traveled. But he was steadfast in who he was seeking approval from - God. It led to attempts on his life, threats of and eventual imprisonment and a host of enemies. But Paul was unwavering in his conviction. He was seeking approval from God. And you should too. No matter the outcome. No matter who turns on you. No matter the friends or relationships lost. God's approval is the only one that matters. So when you set out to prove something today, prove it to God. Because He is the only one who matters!

DAY 53

"The reality of heaven doesn't take away the pain or suffering or our losses, but it assures us that our pain is temporary." Dave Dravecky

He will wipe every tear from their eyes and there will be no more death or sorrow or crying or pain. All these things are gone forever. Revelation 21:4

Life is full of trials and tribulations. Pain and suffering are often out of our control. And the tears and heartaches we experience are real. But luckily for followers of Christ, our pain is only temporary. Because heaven is real, too. The New Jerusalem. And when we enter the gates of heaven, there will be no more tears, death and mourning. Suffering will be no more. So hold on. Ask God to be with you during the tearful days you face and look forward to the day that all pain, sorrow and suffering will be nothing more than a distant memory. Because Heaven awaits us all!

DAY 54

"It's a good thing I stayed in Cincinnati for four years - it took me that long to learn how to spell it." Rocky Bridges

Stay here in this land. If you do, I will build you up and not tear you down; I will plant you and not uproot you. Jeremiah 42:10

Americans move more today than ever. For jobs, for family, for changes of environment and sometimes to escape problems and situations that they are facing. If you are thinking about moving or leaving, have you asked God for guidance? And are you willing to accept His answer? In other words, would you be willing to stay if He told you to stay? God instructed the Israelites to remain in Egypt, as He knew they were thinking of leaving. He promised them prosperity and longevity where they were. But they insisted on leaving anyway. Sometimes we act just like the Israelites. We leave when God tells us to stay. We move when we should remain. So if you're contemplating relocation, ask God first. And listen to His answer. He may be telling you to bloom where you are planted!

DAY 55

"Jackie (Robinson) was the greatest competitor I ever saw. He didn't win. He triumphed." Ralph Branca

But thank God! He has made us his captives and continues to lead us along Christ's triumphal procession. 2 Corinthians 2:14a

There's not much that feels better than winning. Victory. It is what we strive for every time we take the field. But even with the best effort and preparation, sometimes our efforts fall short. However, even in defeat, you're still a winner in God's eyes. Even if it doesn't feel like you're winning, find comfort in knowing that God's plan and will for your life will always prevail. In Christ, we will always be victorious. We will always triumph. Today, when you look in the mirror, see yourself as a winner. God does. And that's all that matters!

DAY 56

"Guessing what the pitcher is going to throw is 80% of being a successful hitter. The other 20% is just execution." Hank Aaron

There is more hope for a fool than for someone who speaks without thinking. Proverbs 29:20

Thinking. We were all made with the ability to do it. But so many times we act out of impulse instead of thinking through our actions. And when we do, it often leads to disaster. Hurt feelings. Fractured friendships. Broken relationships. If only we had thought before acting or speaking. Hitting requires thinking and execution. And life does too. So today, before acting or speaking out of impulse, think your situation through and talk to God about it. You'll be glad you did. And so will those around you!

DAY 57

"No one wants to hear about the labor pains, they just want to see the baby."

Lou Brock

It will be like a woman suffering the pains of labor. When her child is born, her anguish gives way to joy because she has brought a new baby into the world.

John 16:20

The process is never easy. There's challenges and difficulties and pain and struggle. We're driven to the point of wanting to throw the towel in and quit. But the end result is always worth it. Always. You see, God uses the events in our lives to mold us and refine us. To give birth to a new and improved You. A Child of God. Similar to the process of labor pains and the birth of a baby, God rejoices every time our character becomes more like Christ. Think of it as a rebirth. We're all "Under Construction." We're all a work in progress. You're not alone. God's at work. And He's always in control!

DAY 58

"I have learned that God's silence to my questions is not a door slammed in my face. I may not have the answers but I do have Him." Dave Dravecky

O God, do not be silent! Do not be deaf. Do not be quiet, O God. Psalms 83:1

Silence. It can be so uncomfortable and deafening. Especially when we think that God is the one being silent. Not speaking to us. Not hearing us. Not answering our prayers. It can be scary and worrisome. But remember, God is constantly at work in your life and He always hears and answers your prayers. But sometimes we don't like the answers. Because "no" and "not yet" are answers that God sometimes gives. For various reasons. To protect. To redirect. To prepare. To teach. Remember, God hears you and He speaks to you. Start this day by asking the Holy Spirit to help you discern His voice. It may be clearer and louder than you thought!

DAY 59

"Close doesn't count in baseball. Close only counts in horseshoes and hand grenades." Frank Robinson

Come close to God, and God will come close to you. Wash your hands, you sinners; purify your hearts, for your loyalty is divided between God and the world. James 4:8

Frank Robinson was right. But he left out one area where close does count. And that's in our relationship with God. God desires a close relationship with each and every one of us. Especially you. But He won't force it. It's up to you. So many times we allow the world to get in the way of our relationship with God. Distractions, noise, outside influences - they all divide our attention. And they distract us from what's important - our relationship with God. So today, wash your hands, purify your heart and draw close to God. See how close you can get to Him. I'll bet He meets you halfway!

DAY 60

"I've come to the conclusion that the two most important things are good friends and a good bullpen." Bob Lemon

A friend is always loyal, and a brother is born to help in time of need.

Proverbs 17:17

A true Christian friend is hard to come by. Someone who will love you in and through any situation. Through the good times and the bad. The mountains and the valleys. The same way God loves us. We were not created to do life alone. We were created for relationships and to be part of the community of Christ. And by putting Christ first in our lives, we are able to be a true friend. Are you a true friend? Or does your friendship waiver, depending on the circumstances? If there's any question, turn to God and ask Him to help you be a true friend. Ask Him to help you be the type of friend you wished you had in your time of need. Your friends will thank you!

DAY 61

"The saddest day of the year is the day baseball season ends."
Tommy Lasorda

The Lord is close to the broken-hearted; he rescues those whose spirits are crushed. Psalms 34:18

Have you ever felt sad, broken-hearted or crushed? If so, you're not alone. We all feel that way from time to time. We all feel like the weight of the world is on our shoulders at some point in our lives. But the good news is that God cares about our sorrows and sadness. He wants to help bear the burden of our pain. And He wants to hear from us in our time of need. All you need to do is ask. Through prayer, ask God to be present with you in the midst of your sadness. To comfort you. Prayer is the place where burdens change shoulders. God's shoulders are stronger and more capable than yours. So give your burdens to Him. Turn your sadness over to God. And be joyful for His presence!

DAY 62

"I think I was the best baseball player I ever saw." Willie Mays

Because of Christ and our faith in him, we can now come boldly and confidently into God's presence. Ephesians 3:12

There's nothing wrong with self confidence. Believing that you are the best, or at the very least, one of the best, goes a long way in competitive situations. In fact, it's necessary for success in many areas of life, especially on the baseball field. But the same confidence that we possess going on the field is the same confidence we should have when approaching God. In prayer and in worship. Jesus gave his life for the sacrifice of our sins. And by accepting Jesus as Lord of our life, we can boldly go before God without any reservation or hesitation. Our faith provides the way. God loves you. He cares about what you're going through. And He always has an "open door policy." You don't have to knock. You don't need to be timid. Approach God with confidence, knowing that He wants to be in constant communication with you - today and always!

DAY 63

"A baseball game is simply a nervous breakdown divided into 9 innings."

Earl Wilson

For God has not given us a spirit of fear and timidity, but of power, love and self discipline. 2 Timothy 1:7

Baseball can be nerve racking. So can life. Both will have you on the edge of your seat. And both will make you want to go into hiding at times! But that's not the way God made us. We weren't made to be timid and fearful. It's inevitable that we will experience those feelings from time to time. But God doesn't want you to approach your days or your life that way. He has filled you with His power and His love. And He has given you the ability to be self disciplined when feelings of timidity and fearfulness begin creeping in. The next time your feelings start to spiral out of control, call on God. Because even though things seem out of control, remember who is actually in control. And for that, we give thanks!

DAY 64

"You don't save a pitcher for tomorrow. Tomorrow it may rain." Leo Durocher

So don't worry about tomorrow, for tomorrow will bring it's own worries. Today's trouble is enough for today. Matthew 6:34

Win today's game today. Win the day, today. So often we become focused and stressed about the future. And when we do, we lose focus for today. We are called to live life one day at a time. Worrying about tomorrow does us no good. In fact, it only hurts us.Trying to solve tomorrow's problems with today's strength is counterproductive. God provides our needs day by day. God is with us in the here and now. And He'll be there tomorrow when it becomes today. So focus on God today. Be a light for someone today. And focus on tomorrow when you wake up tomorrow morning!

DAY 65

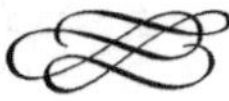

"I was such a dangerous hitter I even got intentionally walked in BP."

Casey Stengel

He (David) sang, The Lord is my rock, my fortress, and my savior; my God is my rock, in whom I find protection. He is my shield, the power that saves me, and my place of safety. He is my refuge, my savior, the one who saves me from violence. 2 Samuel 22:2-3

The intentional walk. Forever useful to set up a matchup advantage. Or to bypass a hot and dangerous hitter. Wouldn't it be nice if we could do the same thing when we are confronted with danger? Dangerous people, dangerous situations, dangerous thoughts? We can. And He's only a prayer away. God is ready, willing and able to help us in dangerous times. We just have to call on Him. He protects us. From others and from ourselves. He is your refuge. He is your fortress. He is your intentional walk. And instead of being your last option when you don't know what else to do, make God your first option today. You'll be glad you did!

DAY 66

"I've only been doing this for 54 years. With a little experience, I might get better." Harry Caray

Wisdom belongs to the aged, and understanding to the old. Job 12:12

None of us are born wise. None of us are born with understanding. It takes time and experience. Lots of it. And unfortunately, sometimes the life experience we need to gain wisdom and understanding can be painful. And heart breaking. But God uses these experiences in our lives to instill wisdom and understanding within us so that we may become a blessing to others. If we allow Him. A mistake is not a bad thing if we can learn from it and grow from it. Are you facing difficult circumstances in your life? Are you attempting to "pick up the pieces" from a devastating moment in the past? If so, ask God to help you grow from it. Ask Him to help you learn from your experience, to gain wisdom from your experience so that you may become the person He has called you to be. Ask God to use your trials for

His glory, so that you may be a blessing to someone else, so that your words of wisdom and understanding can help someone else who desperately needs it!

DAY 67

"It breaks your heart. It is designed to break your heart. The game begins in spring when everything else begins again, and it blossoms in the summer, filling the afternoons and evenings, and then as soon as the chill rain comes, it stops and leaves you to face the fall alone." A. Bartlett Giamatti

So be strong and courageous! Do not be afraid and do not panic before them. For the Lord your God will personally go ahead of you. He will be with you; he will neither fail you or abandon you. Deuteronomy 31:6

Life is full of ups and downs. Ebbs and flows. Excitement and disappointment. And oftentimes, our experiences leave us feeling alone. Feelings of loneliness can lead us down paths of depression and isolation. But today's scripture gives us hope. Hope for better days. Hope for courage and strength. And hope that we will never be alone. Because God will always be with you. Regardless of what you're facing, no matter what you're feeling, God promises to never abandon you. So talk to Him about your loneliness. Take your feelings to Him. Nothing is too big or small for our God. Rest in His presence and experience true comfort and peace. Today and always!

DAY 68

"I'm convinced that every boy, in his heart, would rather steal 2nd base than an automobile." Tom Clark

If you are a thief, quit stealing. Instead, use your hands for good hard work, and then give generously to others in need. Ephesians 4:28

Stealing is an excellent strategy in baseball. But not in life. Getting ahead by stealing is a sin. Taking what someone else has worked hard for, for something not earned or worked for is a terrible way to live. No matter how big or small the item is. It's wrong. In Ephesus, theft was an issue. In fact, some of Paul's readers supported themselves by stealing, which is why he addressed it in his letters. In addition to admonishing their behaviors, Paul implored them to quit and change their ways. Quit stealing. Work hard. And give to those who need it most. Changing habits and our way of life can be difficult. Especially if it's a way of survival. But there's a better way - working hard. And it can benefit others when you follow through and help those who need it most. If you are taking anything that doesn't belong to you, or feeling tempted to do so, ask God to help you. Change your thoughts, change your plans. And change your way of life!

DAY 69

”You either get better or you get worse. Those are the only two options.”

Max Scherzer

Seek the Kingdom of God above all else, and live righteously, and he will give you everything you need. Matthew 6:33

Self help strategies. Self help books. They are literally everywhere. Everyone has an opinion on how you can improve and become the best version of you. But there's only one true way to accomplish this. And that is by seeking the Kingdom of God and a relationship with God, through Christ Jesus. When you strive to know God on a deeper, more personal level, your life becomes richer, more fulfilling and more meaningful. Nothing else will ever accomplish this, no matter the promises made. When your life is devoted to glorifying God, the quality of your life naturally improves. And so do the lives of those around you! So put down the self help books and pick up a Bible. Read it daily. And experience the power of God!

DAY 70

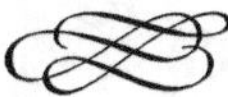

"Nobody ever won the pennant without a star shortstop." Leo Durocher

Those who are wise will shine as bright as the sky, and those who lead many to righteousness will shine like the stars forever. Daniel 12:3

Ever wonder what it takes to be a star? In sports, business, school, life or in the Kingdom of God? Well here's your answer! Leading others to Christ, to a life of righteous living! This is how to become a star! If your goal in life is to be a star, there's only one way to accomplish it. Tell others about Christ, pray for them, encourage them, teach them. And when you do, you'll be a star on God's team - forever!

DAY 71

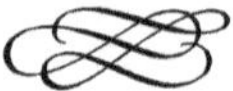

"Baseball players are smarter than football players. How often do you see a team penalized for too many men on the field?" Jim Bouton

If you need wisdom, ask our generous God, and he will give it to you. He will not rebuke you for asking. James 1:5

Have you ever been faced with a difficult decision? Which path to take? What's the best choice? Which direction should I go? Sometimes we are faced with decisions and don't know what to do. Ask God for wisdom when making these tough decisions. When you do, God will grant you the wisdom needed to make the best decision. Asking God demonstrates trust in Him. And luckily for us, when we ask, God gives abundantly and generously, without looking at our track record or past mistakes. So ask Him. Trust Him. And patiently wait for His generous gifts!

DAY 72

"The only thing worse than a Mets game is a Mets doubleheader."

Casey Stengel

Instead of shame and dishonor, you will enjoy a double share of honor. You will possess a double share of prosperity in your land and everlasting joy will be yours. Isaiah 61:7

Twice as nice. Or according to Casey Stengel, twice as bad. It's truly a matter of perspective. Life is full of suffering and discouragement which often leads to shame and embarrassment. But today's scripture reminds us that those feelings should not define us because there are better days ahead. Instead, we are defined by God's love for us. His grace and His mercy. Your suffering is only temporary but God's love is everlasting. And because of this love, you will be blessed. You will be fulfilled. And you will be redeemed. More than you ever could imagine. Thanks be to God!

DAY 73

"Winning is a habit." Leo Durocher

And let us not neglect our meeting together, as some people do, but encourage one another, especially now that the day of his return is drawing near.

Hebrews 10:25

Habits. Some are good. Some are bad. Some are easy to develop but hard to break. What are your habits? Your daily routines? Are you in the habit of spending time with God? With meeting with other believers? Of encouraging others? If these aren't your daily habits, they should be. Habits take time to develop. So do relationships. Take time to grow in your relationship with God. Make spending time with God a daily habit. Your winning habit. Today and every day!

"In the great department store of life, baseball is in the toy department."

Author Unknown

So I decided there is nothing better than to enjoy food and drink and to find satisfaction in work. Then I realized that these pleasures are from the hand of God. Ecclesiastes 2:24

Baseball is fun. It brings us great satisfaction, no matter whether we are playing, coaching or watching it. There are other things in life that can bring us great joy as well. But there is no amount of pleasure or satisfaction that will ever last in our lives, apart from God. We experience true joy in life when we are rooted in God's love. When you view life as a gift from God, you are able to enjoy all aspects of your life. The ups, the downs, the good and the bad. Because you know God is in control as well as the source of all blessings and enjoyment. Abide in Him today and enjoy the pleasures of life!

DAY 75

"All I remember about my wedding day in 1967 is that the Cubs lost a doubleheader." George Will

But when the Father sends the Advocate as my representative- that is, the Holy Spirit- he will teach you everything and will remind you of everything I have told you. John 14:26

As we journey through life, sometimes our memories fail and sometimes our memories fade. Sometimes we forget what we were going to say. And sometimes we forget what we ate for lunch earlier in the day. Remembering can be a challenge. But we should never forget the life and teachings of Jesus. The words He spoke. The way He lived. The way He called all of us to live. With overbooked schedules and never ending to-do lists, it's easy to forget birthdays and whether we turned off the coffee pot in the morning. But don't forget about Jesus. Remember his ways and strive to make them your ways as well. And if you need help remembering, God sent a helper. The Holy Spirit. Thanks be to God!

DAY 76

"We made too many wrong mistakes." Yogi Berra

These things happened to them as examples for us. They were written down to warn us who live at the end of the age. 1 Corinthians 10:11

Mistakes. We all make them. Some are easily corrected. And some are costly and take time to fix. Wouldn't it be nice if we had alarms that sounded right before we made a mistake? Or a warning sign? Would we heed the warning? Because we do have warnings. A whole book full of warnings. The Bible. When facing temptations or decisions in life or things that can greatly impact your life, you should always consult with God. With His Word. With His commands. Learning from your mistakes is a good thing. But learning from God and His Word and avoiding the mistakes altogether is better. Choose better. Choose the Bible.

DAY 77

"Slump? I ain't in no slump…I just ain't hitting." Yogi Berra

The more you grow like this, the more productive and useful you will be in your knowledge of our Lord Jesus Christ. 2 Peter 1:8

A slump is defined as a "sudden severe or prolonged fall in the value or amount of something." We all go through slumps. In baseball. In business. In life. When we aren't as productive as we are expected to be. But slumps are obviously never the goal. We want to be productive, useful and exceed expectations. So how do you accomplish this? By responding to God's promises. By supplementing your faith in God with self-control, patient endurance, brotherly affection and with love for everyone. And when you do, you become productive and useful. And those slumps will only be temporary!

DAY 78

"If I were on the field, I'd want my manager sticking up for me. Sometimes players are dead wrong, ranting and raving, but you stick up for them. They appreciate that." Bobby Cox

Everyone who acknowledges me publicly here on earth, I will also acknowledge before my Father in heaven. Matthew 10:32

We all like to know that someone has our back, no matter what we're going through. It makes a difference. Gives us confidence knowing that we're not alone. With Jesus, we're never alone. He sticks up for us. He walks beside us. He always "has our back." The only requirement is that we acknowledge Him before others. That He is the Messiah. That He is Lord of our life and willingly went to the cross as a sacrifice for our sins. Is that too much to ask? Seems like a pretty good deal. Acknowledge Jesus. And He will acknowledge us in heaven. Praise be to God!

DAY 79

"I knew my career was over. In 1965, my baseball card came out with no picture." Bob Uecker

He said, "I cried out to the Lord in my great trouble, and he answered me. I called to you from the land of the dead, and Lord, you heard me." Jonah 2:2

Sometimes we all feel like it's over. Careers. Dreams. Relationships. And endings can be difficult. Troublesome at best. Crushing at worst. So what do we do when we feel like it's over. The same thing Jonah did. We cry out to God. In your time of need, in your times of trouble, call on God. But God shouldn't be your last option. Instead , make Him your first option. And when you do, God will comfort you and give you peace. And He will resurrect you from the land of the dead!

DAY 80

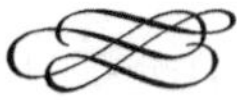

"So I'm ugly. I never saw anyone hit with his face." Yogi Berra

Your beauty should not come from outward adornments, such as braided hair and the wearing of gold jewelry and fine clothes. Instead, it should be that of your inner self, the unfading beauty of a gentle and quiet spirit, which is of great worth in God's sight. 1 Peter 3:3-4

Outward beauty is subjective. What appears beautiful to one, may be flawed to another. But it's not what's on the outside that makes us beautiful in God's eyes, it's our spirit. Is your spirit gentle and quiet? Is your inner self one of peace? Because that's what God finds attractive. No amount of jewelry or expensive clothes can cover up an ugly spirit. It's like putting lipstick on a pig. Outward beauty is a result of inner peace. Be at peace. And be you'll be beautiful in God's eyes. Those are the only eyes that matter!

DAY 81

"Man, this is baseball. You gotta stop thinking." Benny the Jet - The Sandlot

And now, dear brothers and sisters, one final thing. Fix your thoughts on what is true, and honorable, and right, and pure, and lovely, and admirable. Think about things that are excellent and worthy of praise. Philippians 4:8

Do you think too much? Are you an over-thinker? If so, what are you thinking about? Work? School? Family issues? If so, it's time to stop and change the way you're thinking! Over-thinking leads to worry and does you no good. Paul instructs us to "fix our thoughts." Focus your thoughts on what is honorable, right and lovely. These thoughts don't lead to worry. They lead to a full heart and a connected spirit. Thinking about Godly things will brings you into a deeper relationship with God. And that should be your goal every day!

DAY 82

"Fans, for the past two weeks you have been reading about the bad break I got. Yet today, I consider myself the luckiest man on the face of the earth."

Lou Gehrig

Whatever is good and perfect is a gift coming down from God our Father, who created all the lights and heavens. He never changes or casts a shifting shadow. James 1:17

One of the most famous baseball quotes of all time, Lou Gehrig spoke these words following his ALS diagnosis. A terminal disease, it would soon become known as Lou Gehrig's Disease. Yet Gehrig still viewed himself as lucky. What a testimony! Gehrig knew that life was a gift and regardless of what was going on in his life, God was still in control. He knew God never changes. And the same is true for each one of us. God is the same yesterday, today and tomorrow. He doesn't change. His love doesn't waiver. He's still on the throne. Regardless of what you're facing today, your life is still a gift from God. This day is a gift. Approach it with gratitude.

DAY 83

"The only people I ever felt intimidated by in my whole life were Bob Gibson and my daddy." Dusty Baker

Don't be intimidated in any way by your enemies. This will be a sign to them that they are going to be destroyed, but that you are going to be saved, even by God himself. Philippians 1:28

Have you ever been intimidated by someone who was trying to keep you from accomplishing your goals? Were they successful? Intimidation instills fear and suppresses confidence. Intimidation creates doubt - in ourselves, in our mission and in our calling. Intimidation is a tactic used on the field by our opponents and in our lives by the enemy. But God already knew the enemy would use intimidation against us, so He gave us the strength to overcome. Don't be intimidated by your opponent or the enemy. The Spirit of God lives in you. And His power is greater than anything the enemy could ever use against you!

DAY 84

"You have to learn how to get comfortable with being uncomfortable."

Lou Piniella

Then Jesus said to his followers, "If any of you want to be my follower, you must give up your own way, take up your cross and follow me. Matthew 16:24

Life is full of change. And change can be very uncomfortable. We like comfort and we like being in control. But through the uncomfortable changes in our lives, personal growth takes place. Jesus challenged his disciples (and us) to give up our own way and make changes, if we truly want to be His follower. This involves giving up your way of thinking, your way of living and your selfish ambitions. All are things that make us feel comfortable and in control. Following Jesus comes at a cost. It starts by leaving our comfort zone. And trusting where God is leading you. Start today. Follow Jesus, no matter how uncomfortable it may be.

DAY 85

"You trying to say Jesus Christ can't hit a curveball?" Eddie Harris - Major League

Jesus looked at them intently and said, "Humanly speaking, it is impossible. But not with God. Everything is possible with God." Mark 10:27

Hitting a curveball can be difficult. Hitting a good curveball can seem impossible. Fouling it off is sometimes your only hope. It's the same with life as well. Sometimes overcoming difficult situations seems impossible too. And "fouling it off," just trying to get through the day is our only hope. But as we are confronted with adversity, remember that nothing is impossible with God. God is a God of miracles. And He cares for each of us deeply. No matter what you are facing, God is there with you . Coaching you. Leading you. So if all you can do is foul it off, do it. Talk to God. And then swing for the fences!

DAY 86

"I guess I never was in awe of anybody. I think you have to have that attitude if you're going to go far in this game." Bob Gibson

Let the whole world fear the Lord, and let everyone stand in awe of him.

Psalms 33:8

Star-struck. Mesmerized. We live in a world of celebrity worship. Athletes, actors and musicians. So many worship their every move and the words they speak. But there is only that we should be in awe of - God. Our Father in heaven. God's Word is the only word that matters. His approval is the only approval worth seeking. God is to be worshiped and revered. He is to be praised and magnified. No one else deserves our attention and focus. Only God. No one else. Today, instead of checking to see what your favorite celebrity has to say, find out what God has to say. And then follow it. It will take you far!

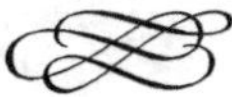

"As long as you live, keep smiling because it brightens everybody's day."

Vin Scully

A cheerful look brings joy to the heart; good news makes for good health.

Proverbs 15:30

A smile is a powerful thing. It can change someone's day. Because everyone has a story. Everyone is dealing with something. Fighting a battle we know nothing about. A smile from you can change everything. Their whole outlook. It's hard to keep smiling sometimes. Life can be hard. But there's someone out there who needs to see your smile today. Someone who needs to be cheered up. Every time you smile, the light of Christ shines through you onto others. So don't stop smiling!

DAY 88

"If we are going to win the pennant, we've got to start thinking we're not as good as we think we are." Casey Stengel

Don't be selfish; don't try to impress others. Be humble, thinking of others as better than yourselves. Philippians 2:3

It's easy for success to go to our heads. On the ball field and in life. Our head gets bigger. Egos inflate. And our self image becomes skewed. We begin thinking that our success, or our team's success, is a direct result of our own individual greatness. And this usually precedes our downfall. Paul's words speak directly to this. Instead of becoming selfish and self centered, Paul reminds us to remain humble and avoid selfish behaviors. In doing so, you will remain hungry for success. No matter where you are. Or what you're doing. In your faith walk. At your job. On the field. God sees your growth and He sees your success. And He sees your attitude towards both. Remember what got you where you are - hunger and humility. Don't stop doing both!

DAY 89

"If you have a bad day in baseball and start thinking about it, you will have 10 more." Sammy Sosa

Don't be dejected and sad, for the joy of the Lord is your strength.

Nehemiah 8:10

Dwelling on mistakes often leads to more mistakes. Thinking about an error usually leads to another error. Learn from it. Get better from it. But don't get lost in it. Mistakes and errors happen. Bad days happen. But don't let them affect the next play. Or determine your future. We serve a God that loves us more than we could ever imagine. And He wants to see you succeed. He is the source of your hope and the source of your strength. Through Him, and in Him, we grow from our mistakes. We learn from our mistakes. But never should we dwell on them. So today, ask God to forgive you for your misstep, to help you grow from it and learn from it. And be joyful knowing that He will!

"Baseball is not a sport you can achieve individually." Curt Schilling

Yes, the body has many different parts, not just one part. 1 Corinthians 12:14

Baseball is truly a team sport. A collection of individuals working together to achieve a collective goal through hard work, well executed strategies, study and preparation. No one player can win a game. Or a championship. It takes everyone on the roster contributing. And it's the same way with the body of Christ. It's true - we can accomplish great things individually for the Kingdom of God. But we can accomplish so much more when we work together. When we use the various talents that God has blessed each of us with and use them to spread and demonstrate God's love, lives are changed. People are led to a life in Christ. And souls are won. What is your gift? How can God use you on His team? Take time today to ask God to reveal your talents and use them accordingly!

DAY 91

"Wherever I go, God will be with me." Yasiel Puig

For the Lord your God is living among you. He is a mighty savior. He will take delight in your gladness. With his love, he will calm your fears. He will rejoice over you with joyful songs. Zephaniah 3:17

Life can be lonely. Relationships end. Friendships fall apart. Loved ones pass away. It can sometimes feel like we are living on an island. Alone. But we are never alone. No matter how isolated we may feel, God is always with us. Wherever you go, God is there. Holding your hand, leading the way. God is a living God. Living in your heart and alive in the world. And because of this, you should never feel alone. When others leave you, God won't. He remains by your side. Today and every day.

DAY 92

"The game shouldn't be called baseball. It should be called adjustments."

Orel Hershiser

I am the Lord, and I do not change. That is why you descendants of Jacob are not already destroyed. Malachi 3:6

Orel Hershiser is right. Baseball is a game of adjustments. So is life. We live in a world that is constantly changing. Nothing ever remains the same. Except for God. He is the one and only constant. His love for us remains the same. And this verse is a reminder. When relationships, finances and jobs change, God's love doesn't. He is always there. Tender, merciful and forgiving. Your plans may change today. It may lead to disruption and frustration. But God's ever loving presence will never change.

DAY 93

"When you think positive, good things happen." Matt Kemp

Yet I am confident I will see the Lord's goodness while I am here in the land of the living. Psalms 27:13

Approaching an at bat with a negative mindset usually leads to a strikeout. Or at the very least, an out. The same is true in life. Positive thoughts often lead to positive results. Entering into your day with a positive outlook is a key to success. It's also an important aspect of our faith. Confidence demonstrates trust in God's promises. His promise to never leave us or never forsake us. He is a good God. He is a God of hope, love and mercy. And He wants to shower you with His blessings! How confident are you that you will experience God's goodness today? Be confident. Think positive. And experience the goodness of God!

DAY 94

"That's why I don't talk. Because I talk too much." Joaquin Andujar

Whoever keeps his mouth and tongue, keeps himself out of trouble.

Proverbs 21:23

Sometimes it's hard to stay quiet. Sometimes it's impossible. But it often leads to trouble. Ill timed jokes. Saying the wrong thing in the wrong tone at the wrong time. Sharing too much. If only we could have remained silent in the moment. But silence requires self control. And self control is challenging. For all of us. But our scripture today reminds us of the importance of guarding our mouth and our tongue. In doing so, we avoid trouble. We avoid embarrassment. We avoid regret. Today, ask God to help you watch your words. And when you do speak, ask Him to give you the right words to say.

DAY 95

"I exploit the greed of all hitters." Lew Burdette

But people who long to be rich fall into temptation and are trapped by many foolish and harmful desires that plunge them into ruin and destruction.

1 Timothy 6:9

Swinging for the fences when all the team needs is a ground ball to the right side. A greedy mindset. A me first mentality. The results are usually less than desirable. Leads to chasing pitches out of the zone, stranded base runners and missed scoring opportunities. Greed in life is similar. When we begin chasing riches, our journey is filled with destruction. Ruined relationships. Hurt feelings. And missed opportunities. Opportunities to love and opportunities to serve. When you are too focused on becoming rich, you lose focus on what's really important - your relationship with God. Greed can lead to questionable decision making and bad choices. So instead of chasing money, chase God. Pursue Him at all cost, starting today.

DAY 96

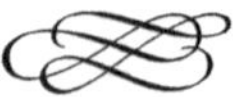

"You owe it to yourself to be the best you can be - in baseball and in life."

Pete Rose

So if your hand or foot causes you to sin, cut it off and throw it away. It's better to enter eternal life with only one hand or one foot than to be thrown into eternal fire with both of your hands and feet. Matthew 18:8

Being the best version of ourselves is something that we should always strive for, no matter where we are or what we're doing. But sometimes it's much easier said than done. Outside factors, outside influences. Things that are out of our control. They can all interfere with our quest for being the best we can be. But what about the things you can control? Those habits, thoughts and actions that derail the best you. Jesus is quite direct with his words. If there are things in your life that interfere with your relationship with God, get rid of them! No matter what it may be. Ask God today to help you remove whatever is preventing you from being the best you that you can be, as well as anything that is interfering with your relationship with Him. You owe it to yourself. And you'll be glad you did!

DAY 97

"I don't care how long you've been around, you'll never see it all."

Bob Lemon

So we don't look at the troubles we can see now; rather, we fix our gaze on things that cannot be seen. For the things we see now will soon be gone, but the things we cannot see will last forever. 2 Corinthians 4:18

Close your eyes. What do you see? Do you see the things that trouble you? Things that cause pain and sadness in your life? Or do you see God's goodness and blessings? What you see and focus on will greatly influence your attitude throughout your day. And throughout your life. Be aware of the things that trouble you. Ask God to guide you through your circumstances. But don't dwell on them. For they will be short lived. Instead, focus your thoughts on God. The comfort He provides. And the hope He promises. Those things that can't be seen but will last forever - unlike your troubles.

DAY 98

"Never make predictions, especially about the future." Casey Stengel

Look here, you who say, "Today or tomorrow we are going to a certain town and will stay there a year. We will do business there and make a profit." How do you know what your life will be like tomorrow? Your life is like the morning fog - it's here a little while, then it's gone. James 4:13-14

There's a difference between making goals in life and making predictions for our lives. Making personal goals is important. But predicting where our lives will go can be disappointing. Because we don't know how our life will play out. When you try to predict how things will go, you often try to take control of your life instead of letting God remain in control. And that's what's important. Allowing God to be in control. Trusting Him. Following Him. Being led by His Holy Spirit. Don't make predictions. Make goals. Be flexible. Trust God. And follow wherever He leads you.

DAY 99

"Fans don't boo nobodies." Reggie Jackson

In the very place where they were once named Nobody, they will be named God's Somebody. Hosea 1:10

Reggie was right. Fans don't boo nobodies. You've got to be a somebody to be booed. Someone who has accomplished a lot - usually against their team. In a strange way, it's almost a sign of respect. But in life, none of us are nobodies. In God's eyes, we are all somebody. We are His children. And regardless of your past, your mistakes and your missteps, you should never feel like a nobody. God created each of us. He is proud of you. He loves you. You are somebody. You are His!

DAY 100

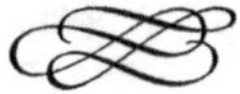

"You better cut the pizza into 4 pieces because I'm not hungry enough to eat 6."

Yogi Berra

Jesus replied, "I am the bread of life. Whoever comes to me will never be hungry again. Whoever believes in me will never be thirsty. John 6:35

Hunger can be painful. Prolonged hunger can lead to death. But Jesus offers Himself as the bread of life. A guarantee that we will never be hungry again. Or thirsty again. We only need to believe in Him. To come to Him. And make Him Lord of our lives. The bread of life is free. It doesn't cost us a thing. But it cost Jesus His life. It was purchased with love, so you will never be hungry or thirsty again!

DAY 101

"You can observe a lot just by watching." Yogi Berra

Therefore keep watch, because you do not know on what day your Lord will come. Matthew 24:42

People watching. To some, it's an odd way to pass time. But to others, it's highly entertaining. But either way, everyone can agree, Yogi was right. You really can "observe a lot by watching!" Jesus actually instructs us to keep watch. To be alert. To stay awake. For the return of the Lord will come at an unexpected time. And you must be aware. Of your actions, your words and your thoughts. This life is only temporary but your next life is eternal. And your next life can start without warning. So be watchful. Be observant. And be obedient. To Jesus's teachings. And the presence of God. Amen!

DAY 102

"How can you think and hit at the same time?" Yogi Berra

The Lord will help you understand all these things. 2 Timothy 2:7b

Our thoughts can be confusing. And troubling. And trying to figure them out and whether or not to act, can be exhausting. Turning to God in these confusing moments is truly the only option. Paul instructs Timothy on how to be strong in his teaching and in spreading of the Gospel. His words are deep and full of wisdom. Paul then tells Timothy to think about what he has said and lean on God for clarity and understanding. Good advice for all of us. Thinking too much can be detrimental. Asking God for direction never is. Today, ask Him for help deciphering your thoughts. And for the strength to act on the ones that are aligned with His will.

DAY 103

"Everybody gets one chance to do something great. Most people never take the chance." Spirit of Babe Ruth - The Sandlot

Make the most of every opportunity in these evil days. Ephesians 5:16

Each day and each moment is a gift from God. Are you making the most of it? Time flies. Days pass. And there's no way to get them back. Once they're gone, they're gone. So are you choosing to live each day to the fullest? Or do you live your days full of regret? The would've, should've and could've of life. Every day we are presented with opportunities to make a difference, to spread the Gospel, to do something great. Do you welcome these opportunities? Or do you let them pass by? Seize every opportunity to make a difference. To serve God. To allow the light of Christ to shine through you onto the paths of others. Be great. Today. And every day.

DAY 104

"Do you know how good you have to be to strike out 2000 times?"

Casey Stengel

"Why do you call me good?" Jesus asked. "Only God is truly good."

Mark 10:18

Great success often comes with great failure. To strike out 2000 times in a career signifies a long career and a lot of at-bats. Which only happens if you're good. We are quick to label others as good. In baseball, in sports, in life, in general. But Jesus asks us to consider who deserves to be called good. For only God is good. And no matter how good we are, all of us are sinners. But that doesn't mean you stop striving to be more Christ-like. But no matter how hard you try, you will, indeed, fall short. You will fail. And if you're lucky, you'll fail a lot more than 2000 times!

DAY 105

"It was all I lived for, to play baseball." Mickey Mantle

My old self has been crucified with Christ. It is no longer I who live, but Christ lives in me. So I live in this earthly body by trusting in the Son of God, who loved me and gave himself for me. Galatians 2:20

What do you live for? What is it that motivates you each and every day? Is it your job? Success? Money? Or is it your identity in Christ Jesus? You are called to live for Christ. Because He died for us. Christ is alive in each of us. And that is why we live. It's what we live for. Allowing others to experience the love of Christ, because He loved us first. Motivation can be hard to find. But you don't need to look any farther than the cross. Jesus's crucifixion gives all of us something to live for - Him!

DAY 106

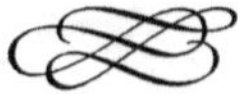

"You make your own luck. Some people have had bad luck all their lives."

Casey Stengel

The trustworthy person will get a rich reward, but a person who wants quick riches will get into trouble. Proverbs 28:20

It is true. We often create our own luck. Both good luck and bad luck. Through our choices and our decisions, we put ourselves in position for good things to happen to us. Or bad things to happen to us. What type of choices are you making? Are your decisions putting you in position for good things to happen to you? Your thoughts, your actions and your words? If so, keep it up. If not, it's time to re-evaluate your decision making process. Ask God to guide your choices. By doing so, you will put yourself in position to receive the blessings God has in store for you. And you'll realize, it's not luck, it's a blessing!

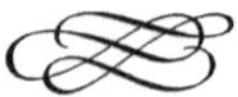

"Heroes get remembered, but legends never die." Spirit of Babe Ruth - The Sandlot

I give them eternal life, and they will never perish. No one can snatch them away from me. John 10:28

Becoming a legend isn't easy. In fact, very few can ever achieve "legendary" status and live forever. In baseball or in life. But eternal life, on the other hand, is very attainable. Not by your own doing, however. There is nothing you can do to grant yourself eternal life. You can't earn it. Can't win it. You can only receive it as a gift. God's gift. And it's for each one of us. By making Jesus Lord of our lives, we inherit eternal life. It can never be taken away. Ever. So today, do something legendary. Accept Him. Tell others about Him. And share in the joy of eternal life!

DAY 108

"When I gave up me, I became more." Don Mattingly

He must become greater and greater, and I must become less and less.

John 3:30

Another interpretation of this verse is, "He must increase, but I must decrease." In other words, less of me, more of Him. John the Baptist was called to tell others about Jesus. And to follow Jesus. For him to do this, however, John had to humble himself so he could be filled with the Spirit of God instead of his own ego. The same is true for us. We are messengers. We are called to share the Good News, which requires humility. Today, ask God to fill you with the Holy Spirit so you may serve Him accordingly. But make sure there's room by decreasing yourself!

DAY 109

"We all have the temptation to be backseat drivers when it comes to decisions that don't work out the way we want." Don Mattingly

In peace I will lie down and sleep, for you alone, O Lord, will keep me safe.

Psalms 4:8

Have you ever been kept awake at night, second guessing a decision you made? One that didn't work out like you hoped? We all have. We stress ourselves out thinking about what we should have done differently. Second guessing ourselves is sometimes second nature. Try not to. Remember that God is still in control. Even in the midst of your bad decisions, He's still on the throne. Which means you can lie down and sleep in peace, without second guessing yourself or the outcome!

DAY 110

"I'm not afraid to be lonely at the top." Barry Bonds

Turn to me and have mercy, for I am alone and in deep distress. Psalms 25:16

It can be lonely at the top. And it can be lonely at the bottom. It can be lonely no matter where we are. David knew that feeling in our scripture today. And his response to feeling alone should be ours as well. Call on God to have mercy on us in our distress. We know that He is always with us, but feelings of loneliness can still creep in. The next time you feel lonely, turn to God. He's only a prayer away!

DAY 111

"I'm not trying to fit in with nobody. I'm just me." Bryce Harper

The world would love you as one of its own if you belonged to it, but you are no longer part of the world. I chose you to come out of the world, so it hates you.

John 15:19

Who are you trying to fit in with? Who do you seek approval from? Teammates? Coworkers? Friends? Or is it God? Trying to fit in with the world will lead you down wrong paths. You may be accepted and celebrated by those around you, but is that your goal? God has set us apart as believers. You are called to be like Jesus, not like the rest of the world. Standing firm in your faith may lead to ridicule. It may lead to isolation. Jesus faced hardships and mockery for His teachings, too. But He was set apart and called to a higher purpose. You are too. So today, be more like Jesus and less like the world!

DAY 112

"I never think about a homer. I'm just thinking of the situation and what I've got to do when I go to the plate." Sammy Sosa

So prepare your minds for action and exercise self control. Put all your hope in the gracious salvation that will come to you when Jesus Christ is revealed to the world. 1 Peter 1:13

Being prepared is important. No matter what you're facing, being prepared is a key to a successful outcome. When we are focused on God and our hope and faith is placed in Him, we are prepared for whatever comes our way throughout the day. Instead of thinking about the possible outcomes, whether good or bad, think about God and His mercy and grace. In doing so, you will find that nothing you face is too big for God. You'll always be ready. And you'll worry less about the outcome and more on Him and His presence. And that's the way it should be!

DAY 113

"I have fun every day. The game is supposed to be fun."
Manny Ramirez

So I recommend having fun, because there is nothing better for people in this world than to eat, drink and enjoy life. That way, they will experience some happiness along with all the hard work God gives them under the sun. Ecclesiastes 8:15

Are you having fun every day? Are you enjoying your life? You should. That's how God intended it to be. It doesn't mean that life will be easy. It doesn't mean that life will be one big vacation. But it does mean that you are supposed to enjoy your time here on earth. That you should look forward to each day, regardless of what you are facing. When you rely on God as your source of joy, life can be fun. It can be enjoyable. So in the midst of your hard work and unpredictable circumstances, have fun. Lean on God. And enjoy your day! Every day.

DAY 114

"It's called talent. I just have it. I can't explain it. You either have it or you don't."

Barry Bonds

In his grace, God has given us different gifts for doing certain things well.

Romans 12:6a

What are your talents ? What are your God-given gifts? Have you recognized them yet? We all have them. We all have gifts and abilities. The problem is, many people never use their talents. Are you one of those people? If so, it's time to change. It's time to use the talents that God has blessed you with. Some people are talented writers, speakers, athletes and teachers. Maybe your talent is something else. Our talents are as unique as we are. God blessed you with talents so they can be used to impact the lives of others. So they can bring joy to others. When you use your gifts, God is glorified. Ask God to reveal your talents to you. Ask Him to put you in a position to use them and then thank Him for it.

And always remember that your talent is a good gift from our good God!

DAY 115

"I like the challenge. I do not like the attention." Pedro Martinez

Dear brothers and sisters, when troubles of any kind come your way, consider it an opportunity for great joy. James 1:2

Do you embrace the challenges in your life? Those unexpected troubles and difficulties that come out of nowhere and blindside you? Sounds crazy, doesn't it? But Today's scripture tells us we should view them as opportunities for great joy. And great growth. Life is hard. Doctor's appointments don't go like we want. Bosses are too demanding. Neighbors are impossible to deal with. We've all been there. But by embracing these challenges and trusting in God's promises, these challenges can quickly become victories. They can become opportunities to develop endurance and strength. But it's all about how you approach your challenges. Embrace them. Trust in God. And claim victory today!

DAY 116

"If people aren't laughing at your goals, they're too small."
Bryce Harper

He (Jabez) was the one who prayed to the God of Israel, "Oh, that you would bless me and expand my territory! Please be with me in all that I do, and keep me from all trouble and pain!" And God granted him his request.

1 Chronicles 4:10

Do you dream big? Do you set huge goals for yourself? Jabez did. Nothing much is written about Jabez, other than two verses in the Bible. But we learn a lot about him. Jabez dreamed big. He set big goals. He asked God to help him. And God "granted his request." No goal is too big. No dream is too far-fetched when you ask for God's help and guidance. Friends and family may laugh. Strangers may doubt you. But God won't. No matter how big your goals are, God is bigger. Trust Him. Follow Him. And aim for the moon!

DAY 117

"I think about baseball when I wake up in the morning. I think about it all day and I dream about it at night. The only time I don't think about it is when I'm playing it."

Carl Yastrzemski

Think about the things of heaven, not the things of earth. Colossians 3:2

We naturally think about what's important to us. Loved ones, jobs, games, the list goes on. Carl Yastrzemski thought about baseball. A lot. It was something that was important to him. What do you spend your time thinking about? What thoughts fill your mind each day? Paul instructs us to keep our thoughts on "the things of heaven." God's goodness. His faithfulness. His love for us. In doing so, you'll be thinking about what really matters. The important things in life. Ask God to help you direct your thoughts towards Him. No matter where you are or what you're doing or facing, focus your thoughts on Him!

DAY 118

"Baseball is such a tough game. It really humbles you at times, you just have to try not to get too high or too low." Chase Utley

For those who exalt themselves will be humbled, and those who humble themselves will be exalted. Luke 14:11

Success can be intoxicating. It can lead to inflated egos and self-promotion. And when we see it in others, we notice it right away. But what about when we see it in ourselves? Do we notice it? Do we see it as a problem? Or do we justify it and continue to let our heads swell? Jesus teaches that we should eliminate all signs of self pride and instead humble ourselves and allow God to do the exalting and promotion. Jesus is the ultimate example of humility. He didn't cling to His status as the Son of God in an attempt to gain favor. Instead, He humbled Himself and remained obedient to God. And at the appropriate time, God exalted Him. Pride is selfish. Pride takes credit and it can be destructive. Ask God to remove pride from your life. Remain humble. And in due time, God will exalt you!

DAY 119

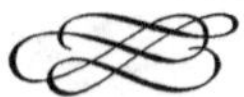

"Baseball is about talent, hard work and strategy. But at the deepest level, it's about love, integrity and respect." Pat Gillick

And you yourself must be an example to the young doing good works of every kind. Let everything you do reflect the integrity and seriousness of your teaching. Titus 2:7

Love, integrity and respect. According to Pat Gillick, these things are essential to the game of baseball. And according to Paul, they are essential to our Christian walk and faith, as well. We have a responsibility to ourselves and to others. To conduct ourselves in a manner that is in line with the teachings of Jesus Christ. "Do as I say, not as I do" is not an option. What you say and what you do must be in line with one another. Young people are watching. Friends are watching. Non-believers are watching. And because of this, your words and actions matter. Be consistent. And be the light that our fallen world so desperately needs!

DAY 120

"When you come to a fork in the road, take it." Yogi Berra

Seek his will in all you do, and he will show you which path to take.

Proverbs 3:6

Following directions from Yogi must have been confusing! Choosing paths and directions in our own life can be confusing as well. Where to live, which job offer to accept, what to do with our lives; there's so many choices to make. It seems we come to a fork in the road every day. But when you seek out God's will, when you seek to know Him more and more each day, your paths become clearer. And your anxiety becomes less. God reveals Himself as we grow in relationship with Him. And when He does, you will come to a better understanding of where God is leading you. Seeking God's will is something you should do every day, not just just the days filled with tough decisions!

DAY 121

"I said I'm going to hit the next one right over the flagpole. God must have been with me." Babe Ruth

Look! The virgin will conceive a child! She will give birth to a son, and they will call him Immanuel, which means God with us. Matthew 1:23

There's no doubt that God was with Babe. And there's no doubt that He's with you as well. Every day. Everywhere you go. Life is always changing! And because of God's presence, we no longer have to live in fear, alienation or with anxiety. You are never alone. There is no reason to fear. The creator of the universe is always with you! No matter what situation you find yourself in, God is already there. Fighting your battles. Finding a way. His Way.

DAY 122

"The way a team plays as a whole determines its success. You may have the greatest bunch of individual stars in the world, but if they don't play together, the club won't be worth a dime." Babe Ruth

I appeal to you, dear brothers and sisters, by the authority of our Lord Jesus Christ, to live in harmony with each other. Let there be no divisions in the church. Rather, be of one mind, united in thought and purpose.

1 Corinthians 1:10

We live in a culture where individuality is valued, marching to the beat of our own drum is promoted and being your own person is thought of as best. And while we are a collection of individuals with different personalities, gifts and goals, let us not forget that we are all members of the same team - God's team. Just like any sports team, our success as members of God's team is directly proportional to our willingness to work together, set our differences aside and come together as one. Whereas a sports team's goal is winning games, ours is introducing others to Jesus through our words and actions and glorifying God in all that we do. Let's play like a team, starting today!

DAY 123

"You've got to give the other man his chance. That's why this is the greatest game." Earl Weaver

Jesus told him, "I am the way, the truth, and the life. No one can come to the Father except through me." John 14:6

We are all given chances and opportunities in life. Chances to further our education, chances to improve professionally, chances to be a better person. What you do with your chances is up to you. Do you make the most of your opportunities? Or do you let them pass by? But there's another opportunity that has been presented to you as well. And that is the chance to spend eternity with our Heavenly Father. To do so, you must accept Jesus as Lord of your life. There is only one way to the Father. And it is through Jesus. Accept Him today. It's the greatest opportunity you'll ever have. And you will never regret it.

DAY 124

"My pitching philosophy is simple - keep the ball away from the bat."

Satchel Paige

The Lord protects those of childlike faith; I was facing death and he saved me. Psalms 116:6

We have a tendency to make life more complicated than it needs to be. Rules, roles, relationships, etc. We sometimes do this with our faith as well. Today's scripture speaks of "childlike faith." Keeping it simple. No over complications. Accept. Believe. Trust. And when you do, you will be saved. Both eternally and from fear and worry. Your relationship with God is simple. He is your Father. You are His child. You are not in control, but He is. It's just that simple.

DAY 125

"Don't let the winds blow your dreams away…or steal your faith in God."

Vin Scully

Faith shows the reality of what we hope for; it is the evidence of things we cannot see. Hebrews 11:1

Faith can be confusing. And complicated. What is faith? Do I have it? And that's why this verse is important. The Bible is full of promises that we cannot see. Stories of people we never knew or met. Part of faith is believing the Bible is real. That God's promises are real. That His goodness and love for us is true. You take other people's words as true. Do the same with God's Word. He loves you and promises to always be there. It's up to you to believe Him. All it takes is a little faith!

DAY 126

"I'm not a guy that sits around and does nothing." Dusty Baker

What good is it, dear brothers and sisters, if you say you have faith but don't show it by your actions? Can that kind of faith save anyone? James 2:14

Laziness in life is a terrible quality to possess. No drive + no goals + no passion = no results. The same formula is true when it comes to our faith. We are called to be active in our faith. We are called to pursue God, to grow our faith and to tell others about the power of the Cross. We are not called to sit in the bleachers and watch other believers do the work. Spiritual laziness is a curse. Claiming to have faith and not showing it is useless. Your faith serves no purpose if you don't show it with your actions. Loving. Serving. Growing. It's part of an active faith. Do your part by sharing it with others!

DAY 127

"If a tie is like kissing your sister, losing is like kissing your grandmother with her teeth out." George Brett

If you try to hang on to your life, you will lose it. But if you give up your life for my sake, you will save it. Luke 9:24

Having a game end in a tie is terrible. Having a game end with a loss is even worse. Nobody likes to lose. When we compete, we play to win. It's why we play. Winning feels good and losing is no fun. But there is one loss that is acceptable. And that is when we lose ourselves, when we give up ourselves, for Christ's sake. Following Jesus requires sacrifice. It requires losing your sense of self, your desire to live for yourself, and choosing to live for God. Because when we lose ourselves, we actually end up winning. Your soul is saved and victory is yours. Because you are His!

DAY 128

"I expect perfection from myself." Bryce Harper

But those who obey God's word truly show how completely they love him. That is how we know we are living in him. 1 John 2:5

Perfection. It's great to strive for but impossible to achieve. We make mistakes. Accidents happen. Unlucky bounces. Bad calls. Plans, performance, people - nothing is perfect. Except God's Word. And when we exhibit obedience to God's Word, our love for Him is put on display. Complete dedication to the teachings of Jesus Christ. Trying to be like Him. The only perfect One. Falling short of perfection is to be expected. It's a goal worth striving for. But a better goal today is to be more like Jesus.

DAY 129

"I'm proof that great things can happen to ordinary people if they work hard and never give up." Orel Hershiser

The members of the council were amazed when they saw the boldness of Peter and John, for they could see that they were ordinary men with no special training in the scriptures. They also recognized them as men who had been with Jesus. Acts 4:13

God wants to use you. Yes, you. No formal training? No worries. No higher education? No problem. Checkered past? Even better. God uses ordinary people to accomplish great things for His Kingdom. And that includes you! When you commit to serving God and growing in relationship with Him, He will put you in position to serve others. He will put you where you're needed. He'll give you the words to say. God can use you. He wants to use you to accomplish extraordinary things for His Kingdom, no matter how ordinary you feel!

DAY 130

"The only place I've found peace in my life is church. I owe my life to God."

Daryl Strawberry

May the Lord bless you and protect you. May the Lord smile on you and be gracious to you. May the Lord show you his favor and give you his peace. Numbers 6:24-26

Peace. We all want it. We look everywhere for it. We move. We change. We quit and start over. But there's only one place where we will ever find peace. Nothing else in life will ever give us peace. In the midst of our busy and stressful lives, God is our source of peace. In the midst of our sorrow and sadness, God is our source of peace. No matter where we are or what we're going through, God is our source of peace. It transcends understanding. There are no words to describe it. Because the peace that God gives is indescribable. Are you experiencing hardship today? Is your heart full of worry and fear? If so, It's time to talk to God. His peace is all you need.

DAY 131

"I have a lot of regrets about what I've done. If I had to do it over again, I never would have left the Mets." Daryl Strawberry

No, dear brothers and sisters, I have not achieved it, but I focus on this one thing: Forgetting the past and looking forward to what lies ahead.

Philippians 3:13

We all have regrets. Actions and words we wish we could take back. Situations where "I'm sorry," doesn't feel like nearly enough. If we could only have a do-over. But God doesn't want you to live with regret about what you've done. Instead, God wants you to come to Him, repent and ask for forgiveness and then move forward. Learn from your mistakes. Work hard to never repeat them. But find peace knowing that you are forgiven. Regret looks back. Hope looks forward. Focus on "what lies ahead."

DAY 132

"Pitching is the art of instilling fear." Sandy Koufax

**But when I am afraid, I will put my trust in you."
Psalms 56:3**

We are all filled with fear from time to time. Of our future, of situations in our lives, of the doctor's report. Even the bravest person experiences fear at some point. It's natural. David wrote this Psalm when he was fearing for his life. His spirit was full of anxiety and sorrow. Yet he knew where to turn. To God. Which is exactly where you should turn when you are experiencing feelings of fear. When we turn to God, and place our trust in Him, our fear turns into faith. Our perspective changes and we realize that God is bigger than our problems. He loves you. He's for you. And trusting in Him allows you to see this. Remember, GOD>your fears!

DAY 133

"You have to be more disciplined every day to get better and learn the game."

Yasiel Puig

No discipline is enjoyable while it is happening - it's painful! But afterward there will be a peaceful harvest of right living for those who are trained in this way. Hebrews 12:11

Discipline is designed to lead to positive changes. To improvements. In behavior and performance. But it isn't easy. Sometimes it's painful. But the results are what motivate us, knowing that better is possible. Sometimes God disciplines us. Sometimes we are required to discipline ourselves. But the intended results are the same. Personal growth. Less TV, more time reading the Bible. Less ice cream at night, more time on the treadmill. Less time with friends, more time practicing. It requires dedication and determination. And patience. Changes and growth don't happen overnight. It takes time. And discipline.

"My main philosophy is that money is a loan from God. I'm in charge of it. I'm responsible for investing it, giving some of it away, providing for my family and protecting it." Orel Hershiser

He did all this so you would never say to yourself, "I have achieved this wealth with my own strength and energy." Remember the Lord your God. He is the one who gives you the power to be successful, in order to fulfill the covenant he confirmed to your ancestors as an oath. Deuteronomy 8:17-18

Money. We all want it. We work hard for it. We spend it. We save it. We give it away. And sometimes we waste it. What is your attitude about money? Is it yours, all yours? Or is it a loan from God? Your answer to these questions will reveal a lot about your attitude towards God. All gifts, including money, are from our Heavenly Father. No matter how hard you think you worked for it, God put you in a position to earn it. And how you respond with your earnings is what matters. We have been instructed to tithe. To give to those in need. To help our neighbors. Our money belongs to God, and we are called to be good stewards. Spend it wisely. Use it for God's Kingdom. It's His anyway. So glorify Him with how you use it!

DAY 135

"The streak has become my identity; it's who I've become." Cal Ripken, Jr.

But the person who is joined to the Lord is one spirit with him.

1 Corinthians 6:17

Identity theft. It happens when someone takes on your identity and runs up debt or makes purchases in your name. It can ruin your credit and take years to clear. But identity theft also takes place when we forget who we are, and more importantly, whose we are. Too many times, we try to find our identity in what we do. Teacher, coach, manager, parent. Sometimes we find our identity in what we've done, both accomplishments and mistakes. But that's not who we are. It's not our identity. We are children of God. Your worth and your value come from your identity in Him. When you seek out your identity in other places, you prevent yourself from doing what God wants for your life. We are one with God. We are one with the spirit. And that is the only place to truly find your identity!

DAY 136

"Playing baseball is not real life. It's a fantasy world...It's a dream come true."

Dale Murphy

Take delight in the Lord, and he will give you your heart's desire. Commit everything you do to the Lord. Trust him, and he will help you. Psalms 37:4-5

We all have dreams and fantasies that we hope will come true. Sometimes they do. Sometimes they don't. And when they don't, we often feel disappointed and let down. But today's scripture offers encouragement when pursuing our dreams and a proper order, as well. We are called to "delight in the Lord." To live in obedience to Him. Commit to Him. Spend time with Him. Because when you do, your desires quickly become His desires. You will want what God wants, both in your life and for the world. When you do this, God will bring it to pass. So keep trusting Him. Ask God to make your desires the same as His desires. And in time, your dreams will come true!

DAY 137

"The best pitchers have a short term memory and a bulletproof confidence."

Greg Maddox

So do not throw away this confident trust in the Lord. Remember the great reward it brings you! Hebrews 10:35

Success in many areas of your life depends on your own self confidence. Believing in ourselves and our abilities is often a determining factor in the outcome of our efforts - especially in sports. We must believe that our preparation and our talents are far superior to that of our opponents. And that it will lead to success. Self confidence is indeed important. However, it's even more important in life to have confident trust in God. Believing that He is greater than any issues you may be facing. God is greater than your challenges. He will never leave you. Remain confident in the Lord and remind yourself how good He is. Of how He has helped you through difficult times before. Your self confidence may waiver from time to time. But don't ever lose confidence in God's goodness! Today, tomorrow and always!

DAY 138

"You know you're pitching well when the batters look as bad as you do at the plate." Duke Snider

Fools think their own way is right, but the wise listen to others. Proverbs 12:15

Life has a way of making us look foolish at times. Or better said, we have a way of making our own selves look foolish at times. We think we know best. That we've got it all figured out. That we know all the answers. That we know what's best. Only to find out that we don't. In doing so, we find ourselves dealing with the aftermath of another mistake, full of shame and feeling foolish. God places people in our lives who are full of wisdom, who have more experience than we do. And who are willing to help us. God has also given us His Word. The Holy Bible is full of wisdom. Full of life changing guidance. Full of teachings and lessons. Foolish mistakes happen. But you can limit those mistakes by listening to the wise ones God has placed in your life. And by studying and trusting in His Word. You'll be wise if you do!

DAY 139

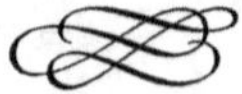

"When you're in a slump, it's almost as if you look out at the field and it's one big glove." Vance Law

Commit your actions to the Lord, and your plans will succeed. Proverbs 16:3

Sometimes in life, it feels like nothing is going right. Like we can't catch a break. We're in a slump that's lasting forever. So how do you break the slump you're in? By refocusing and recommitting your life to the Lord. By trusting in God and His plans for your life. Our best chances for being successful in life are when our plans are aligned with God's Word. When we seek Him and submit to His will, we put ourselves in position for success. Rejecting God and ignoring Him will lead to a life long slump. But trusting in Him and following His will will lead to a life of abundance! Slump or abundance? Which one do you want?

DAY 140

"I managed a team that was so bad we considered a 2-0 count on the batter a rally." Rich Donnelly

When you hear the blast of the trumpet, rush to wherever it is sounding. Then our God will fight for us! Nehemiah 4:20

God is always fighting for you! In the midst of your trials and sorrows, God is fighting your battles. When the enemy is attacking, God is already on the front line defending you. Nothing you face is too big for Him. When you feel surrounded by evil, God steps in. When your back is against the wall, God prepares a way. God's Word is a sword and a light, defeating the enemy and illuminating your path. Call on Him. No matter what you're going through, God is already fighting for you!

DAY 141

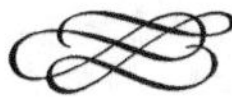

"Regardless of where you're pitching, regardless of what goes on before or after your game, you still have to be ready." Greg Maddox

And now, dear children, remain in fellowship with Christ, so that when he returns, you will be full of courage and not shrink back from him in shame.

1 John 2:28

We're told all our lives to be ready. To be prepared. In sports. In school. At work. In life. But we also must be prepared for the glorious return of Christ. Are you ready? Do you fellowship with Him daily by studying His Word? Do you talk to Him daily through prayer and meditation? Do you seek Him with all your heart? Make your relationship with God your number one priority in life. In doing so, not only will you be ready for the return of Christ, you will be ready for anything life throws at you!

DAY 142

"God isn't really interested in our batting averages." Dale Murphy

But I, the Lord, search all hearts and examine secret motives. I give all people their due rewards, according to what their actions deserve. Jeremiah 17:10

We live in a society that tends to judge people based on their results. Batting average, E.R.A., test scores, sales totals, just to name a few. And based on these results, we label people as "good.". But God isn't as concerned with our results as He is with our motives and our heart. God punishes sin. But He rewards those who place their trust in Him. Those who seek to please Him. Those whose hearts belong to Him. Are your motives pure? Are your words and actions rooted in His love? God knows your heart and you will be judged accordingly. So seek to please Him today and every day!

DAY 143

"Sometimes they write what I say, not what I mean." Pedro Guerrero

Just say a simple, 'Yes, I will,' or 'No, I won't.' Anything beyond that is from the evil one. Matthew 5:37

Say what you mean and mean what you say. If it was only that easy! Sometimes our words get misinterpreted. Sometimes they come out wrong. Sometimes they are used against us. And in the process, feelings are hurt, relationships are damaged and reputations are ruined. Jesus instructs us to keep our words simple. No swearing, no promises, nothing extra. Many conversations and interactions require more than a simple yes or no. If they do, ask God to give you the words to speak and when to say them. In doing so, you can be assured that the words you speak will be full of God's love and peace. And everyone, including you, will be better off!

DAY 144

"My approach to every game was to try to erase the games that were before and try to focus on the game at hand." Cal Ripken, Jr.

This is the day the Lord has made. We will rejoice and be glad in it.

Psalms 118:24

Today. It's all we have. Yesterday is gone. Tomorrow isn't promised. We only have this day. How will you approach it? With hesitation and regret? Or with joy and hope? Today is a gift. God created it just for you. And just like any present, you won't know what's in it until you open it. So open it with excitement, enthusiasm and anticipation. It was made with love and purchased with blood. The way you choose to approach today will greatly influence the outcome. Be joyful, be grateful and be glad. Today is a gift just for you!

DAY 145

"Not many people get to the major leagues and succeed right away. There are some struggles. Everyone seems to struggle." George Brett

The light shines in the darkness, and the darkness can never extinguish it. John 1:5

We have all faced trials and struggles in our lives. Some are tragic, some are less traumatic. But we all experience them. They can leave us anxious, worried and even depressed. Even the most faithful believers can be shaken. But in the darkest of hours, God's light shines brightly. Darkness will never overcome His light. When you are struggling and it seems the darkness is overtaking you, seek out God's light for the world - Jesus. Your struggles are only temporary. God's love and mercies are eternal. Evil will never overcome them. So seek out God's light. Commune with Him. Rest in Him. Struggles will come and go. God doesn't. He's with you forever!

DAY 146

"The other sports are just sports. Baseball is a love." Bryant Gumbel

But anyone who does not love does not know God, for God is love. 1 John 4:8

God is love. Period. It's the very essence of who He is. God first showed us His love by sending His Son to die on the cross for our sins. It's the ultimate act of love and sacrifice. So from the beginning, our relationship with God is rooted in love. And when we truly love God, we act in love towards other people - family, strangers and coworkers. It demonstrates God's love for us. Because love is more than a feeling. It's an action. God acted on His love by sending Jesus. Now it's time to act on our love as well!

DAY 147

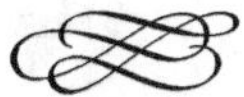

"There are three things in my life which I really love: God, my family and baseball. The only problem - once the season starts, I change the order around a bit."

Al Gallagher

But seek first the kingdom of God and his righteousness, and all these things will be added to you. Matthew 6:33

What are your priorities in life? Where does God rank among your priorities? Is He top five? Did He even make your list? Hopefully, He's number one. If not, it's time to reevaluate your list. Seeking God should always be your top priority. When you spend time with Him daily, reading His Word and communing with Him, everything else on our priority list falls into place. You can approach each day with peace, knowing that God will help put your other concerns in order. Today, choose to put God first. And each day after this, as well.

DAY 148

"A man once told me to walk with the Lord. I'd rather walk with the bases loaded." Ken Singleton

He has told you, O man, what is good; and what does the Lord require of you but to do justice and to love kindness, and to walk humbly with your God? Micah 6:8

What does it mean to walk humbly with God? It means you have a desire to act justly and love mercy. It means you act in kindness and love. It means you never view yourself as better than others. Everyone's walk with God will look different because each of our callings are different. But we are all called to walk with Him. Bases loaded or not, today is your day to walk with God!

DAY 149

"Three more saves and he ties John the Baptist." Hank Greenwald

Truly I say to you, among those born of women there has arisen no one greater than John the Baptist. Yet the one who is least in the kingdom of heaven is greater than he. Matthew 11:11

John the Baptist was a great man. The original saves leader. He spent his life preparing the way and telling others about the coming of Jesus. John wore clothes made of camel hair and ate locusts and honey. Yet he had the honor of baptizing Jesus. An honor he didn't feel worthy of. John the Baptist did great things for the Kingdom of God. Jesus proclaimed there was "no one greater." So why would Jesus then say that "the one who is least in the kingdom of heaven is greater than he?" To give us hope! So that we would know that even those of us who are viewed as "the least" can enter the Kingdom of God. Not by our actions, but by our faith in Christ. And this faith alone will make us greater than John!

DAY 150

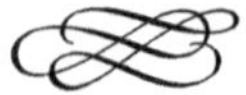

"Bruce Benedict is so slow he'd finish third in a race with a pregnant woman."

Tommy Lasorda

The Lord is compassionate and merciful, slow to get angry and filled with unfailing love. Psalms 103:8

Apparently Bruce Benedict was slow. Really slow. But luckily for us, so is God when it comes to getting angry. Even when we deserve it. When our actions deserve God's wrath, He instead acts in unfailing love. With compassion. Because He loves us. He's merciful. Because He loves us. Despite our sinful nature, despite the times we choose a different path, God's love for you is unfailing. He's patient with you. He knows you are a work in progress. And because of this, your mistakes aren't met with anger. They're greeted with love. Unfailing love. Thanks be to God!

DAY 151

"What happened to me should teach everybody that you should never give up on anybody." David Ortiz

Love is patient and kind. Love is not jealous or boastful or proud or rude. It does not demand its own way. It is not irritable, and it keeps no record of being wronged. 1 Corinthians 13:4

Some of us are "late bloomers" in life and success doesn't come right away. It takes time, lessons learned and do-overs. It takes second chances and second efforts. And even though we may be in a hurry to get "there" (wherever "there" is), God never rushes us. Because of His love for you, He is patient and kind, merciful and forgiving. And that's how you are called to act towards others. God acts in love because He is love. And we are called to act in love as well. When you do, you give others the same opportunity to grow that God gives us. So be patient. Be kind. And love at all times.

<h1 style="text-align:center">DAY 152</h1>

"I live for baseball. That's how I grew up." Joe Buck

If we live, it's to honor the Lord. And if we die, it's to honor the Lord. So whether we live or die, we belong to the Lord. Romans 14:8

We all live for something. Some live for the weekend. Some for Saturday's in the fall with college football. Some live for their families, while others live for their yearly vacation. We all have something that brings us comfort, joy and excitement. Something that keeps us going and motivates us. Today's scripture tells us something else we should live for - honoring God. Whether in life or in death, you belong to Him. And your life should honor Him at all times. When you live to honor God, you will seek to please Him. When you live to honor God, your life will become a reflection of God's love and mercy. And when you do, you will live in peace and harmony with your brothers and sisters. Living for God. It's the only way to live. So what or who will you live for today?

DAY 153

"You never stop learning. You learn something new every day." Robinson Cano

...always learning but never able to come to a knowledge of the truth.

2 Timothy 3:7

We were born to learn. We start learning while still an infant and our learning continues through high school and sometimes through years of college. But our learning shouldn't stop there. Learning is a lifelong endeavor. It's a journey that never ends. And no matter how smart we may feel, we can always learn more. Especially about God's Word and our relationship with Him. In doing so, you will be pursuing truth - God's truth. Some will never learn His truth because of their motives. They are motivated by their own selfish desires and passions, which open the door for false teachings. They are drawn to hearing what they want to hear instead of the truth. Are you still learning? Are your motives pure? Are you drawn to knowing and understanding God's truth? Ask Him to help you. To guide you and lead you through the scriptures. And His truth will be revealed!

DAY 154

"Every great batter works on the theory that the pitcher is more afraid of him than he is of the batter." Ty Cobb

You will keep in perfect peace all who trust in you, all whose thoughts are fixed on you! Isaiah 26:3

Fear can be disruptive. To our lives, our thoughts and our peace. It can overtake our lives and paralyze us. It prevents us from living out the calling God has placed on our lives. Fear can control us and cause countless problems. But fear is the opposite of faith. It's the opposite of trust. You are called to place your trust in God. Always. Especially when you are fearful. When feelings of fear begin to creep in, focus your thoughts on God. Trust in Him. And when you do, you will experience peace. Perfect peace, which is God's peace. Fear is a natural emotion. So let your natural response to a natural emotion be trusting in God. And peace will always be yours!

"Hitting is timing. Pitching is upsetting timing." Warren Spahn

He replied, "The Father alone has the authority to set those dates and times, and they are not for you to know." Acts 1:7

Timing is everything. From saying the right thing at the right time to being in the right place at the right time. It all comes down to timing. Perfect timing can lead to great successes. And epic failures can be the result of bad timing. Unfortunately, we don't always know when the time is right. Or wrong. But God does. He knows what you need and when you need it. He knows when you should speak and when you should listen. He knows when Christ will return and when you will be called home. God knows! Therefore His timing is always perfect! It's up to you to trust in His timing and be obedient to His leading. Perfect trust = perfect timing! Amen!

DAY 156

"I'm a winner. I play to win. I want to make good things go on around me."

David Ortiz

Dear friend, don't let this bad example influence you. Follow only what is good. Remember that those who do good prove that they are God's children, and those who do evil prove that they do not know God. 3 John 1:11

What keeps you from doing good? Busy schedule? Inconvenient? Pressure from social norms? We've all passed up an opportunity to do something good for someone. And oftentimes, we end up regretting it. But more opportunities are coming your way! Don't let anything get in the way or stop you from doing something good for someone else. Living out your faith involves a willingness and commitment to doing good. It often requires sacrifice. But it proves who we are - God's children. God has never hesitated to pour out His goodness on you. So don't ever hesitate to do the same for others!

DAY 157

"You've got to be ready for the fastball." Ted Williams

Remind the believers to submit to the government and its officers. They should be obedient, always ready to do what is good. Titus 3:1

Ted Williams was right. You have to be ready for the fastball. Look for the fastball, adjust to the curve. It's the same in life but not with the pitches. Instead, we should always look to do good and adjust to the opportunities we are presented with. Life is full of uncertainties. You never know what will happen next. But if you are always ready to do good, you can share the love of Christ no matter the circumstances. So today, look for chances to do good and adjust as needed!

DAY 158

"The key to hitting is just plain working at it. Work, that's the real secret."

Ted Williams

The Lord God placed the man in the Garden of Eden to tend and watch over it. Genesis 2:15

Working is part of life. We can't sit around and expect good things to come our way. Even Adam had to work. God placed him in the Garden "to tend and watch over it." Whether working at our jobs or our craft, it requires time and dedication. It requires sacrifice. But the payoff is worth it. Your relationships require work as well. Especially your relationship with God. Following Christ isn't easy. It requires time, dedication and sacrifice. It means giving up your selfish ways and committing to a life that honors God. No matter what you're working at today - your job, your hobby or even your

yard - fully commit yourself. Don't cut corners. Give it your all. And when it comes to your relationship with God, work just as hard. You'll be glad you did!

DAY 159

"He'd give you the shirt off his back. Of course, he'd call a press conference to announce it." Catfish Hunter on Reggie Jackson

Watch out! Don't do your good deeds publicly, to be admired by others, for you will lose the reward from your Father in heaven. Matthew 6:1

Giving and doing good deeds are part of an active faith. Not only are we living out our faith when doing this, we also feel good about ourselves. And who doesn't like to feel good about themselves? The problem becomes our intent. What is your intention when you give and perform good deeds? Is it for the applause from those around us? Or is it to please God? When you seek the recognition of your fellow man, the recognition is your reward. But when your motive is pleasing God, you will be rewarded by Him and blessed by Him. God sees your actions. He sees your motives and knows our intentions. That is what's most important to Him. Your heart. So today, give and perform your good deeds.

Make a difference in the lives of others. But do it for the right reasons and you will be rewarded!

DAY 160

"I believe in rules. Sure I do. If there weren't any rules, how could you break them?" Leo Durocher

Everyone must submit to governing authorities. For all authority comes from God, and those in positions of authority have been placed there by God. Romans 13:1

Are you a rule breaker? Do you like to see how much you can get away with? Do you feel like the rules don't apply to you? Today's verse should serve as a reminder that the rules do matter. And you are called to follow them, regardless of how silly or ridiculous they may be. You are also called to respect your governing authorities, even if you don't agree with their political affiliation. Our leaders have been established by God for His purpose. It's their responsibility to follow God's lead. And it's our responsibility to trust God. Even when our authority figures don't feel loveable, love them anyway. Pray for them. Speak well of them. And respect them. Remember, God put them in their position for a purpose!

DAY 161

"When I broke my arm, I knew there was something a lot bigger than baseball (about to happen)…I had a sense that God had something for me, bigger than baseball." Dave Dravecky

That is what the Scriptures mean when they say, "No eye has seen, no ear has heard, and no mind has imagined what God has prepared for those who love him." 1 Corinthians 2:9

Sometimes life doesn't turn out the way we expected. Sometimes things happen and we don't know why. Sometimes our plans are interrupted and we are left shaking our heads and our fists and asking God "Why?" We don't understand how it could happen. We thought we had it all figured out. But when we are faced with derailed plans, we must find comfort in knowing that God has something else in store for us. God's plan is perfect. His timing is impeccable. God knows what you need when you need it. So trust Him, knowing that He is preparing something for you. Are you dealing with busted plans or derailed dreams? Be patient and trust God. Because as you are reading these words, He's preparing something unimaginable for you!

DAY 162

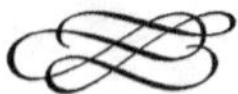

"I get tired of hearing my ballplayers bellyache all the time. They should sit in the press box sometime and watch themselves play." Buzzie Bavasi

Examine yourselves to see if your faith is genuine. Test yourselves. Surely you know that Jesus Christ is among you; if not, you have failed the test of genuine faith. 2 Corinthians 13:5

Self reflection can be difficult. It can be hard. And it can hurt. Because it requires honesty. About ourselves, our habits and our situation. But when you are honest about yourself, great growth and change can take place. How is your spiritual discipline? Do you spend time with God daily? Do you study His Word? Do you give Him thanks in prayer and meditation? Be honest. If the answer is no, acknowledge your shortcomings and ask God to help you. It starts by looking in the mirror and in your heart. Then make a change, starting today!

DAY 163

"The human hand is made complete by the addition of a baseball."

Paul Dickson

My flesh and my heart may fail, but God is the strength of my heart and my portion forever. Psalms 73:26

A baseball may indeed complete the human hand. But it is God who completes us. He is our portion and we are incomplete without Him. Nothing and no one will ever complete us except for God. He provides purpose, healing and fulfillment for our lives. And expecting to find that elsewhere is unrealistic. Where do you find wholeness? In your job? In a relationship? In your hobbies? True wholeness is found in a relationship with Jesus Christ. Seeking to please Him. Seeking an intimate relationship with Him. Spending time with Him. When you do these things, you will be made whole. You will be completed. Without God, your life will always be missing something. And that something is Him. Seek God in all that you do. And you will be made complete.

DAY 164

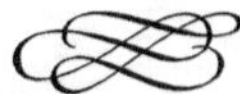

"There are a lot more important things in life than baseball. I just haven't found out what they are yet." Marty Schupak

So now I am giving you a new commandment: Love each other. Just as I have loved you, you should love each other. Your love for one another will prove to the world that you are my disciples. John 13:34-35

Love. The most important thing in life. We are obedient to God's Word when we love. We change lives when we love. And most importantly, we show the world that we are God's children when we love. Jesus's instructions were simple. Love others as He loved us. Who? Everyone. Even those who may seem unlovable. When? Always. Not just when you feel like it or when it's beneficial. It's not a suggestion. It's a new commandment from Jesus. Are you honoring His commandment? Do you love others the same way Jesus loves you? Ask God to help you honor Jesus's words and love everyone. Always and forever, starting today!

DAY 165

"Looking at the ball going over the fence isn't going to help."
Hank Aaron

Accept other believers who are weak in faith, and don't argue with them about what they think is right or wrong. Romans 14:1

Each day we have to make choices and decisions. And one of those decisions involves picking our battles. Deciding who to engage, who to defend and the benefit of the battle. Hank Aaron decided that watching a ball go over the fence wasn't going to help him, his team or the situation. And Paul writes that arguing with other believers about their view of right or wrong won't help us either. As believers, we interpret Scripture to mean different things. But it is not our place to judge their beliefs and interpretations. Instead, you should ask God to be with them on their journey and to open their hearts. If they are wrong, ask God to convict them and change their hearts. And if we are wrong, ask Him to open our hearts as well. Arguing serves no purpose. It benefits no one. So as you go through this day, choose your battles carefully. And let God fight them for you!

DAY 166

"Sandy's fastball was so fast, some batters would start to swing as he was on his way to the mound." Jim Palmer

...The fastest runner doesn't always win the race, the strongest warrior doesn't always win the battle...It is all decided by chance, by being in the right place at the right time. Ecclesiastes 9:11

Speed. It's important in many facets of life. Sports, racing, manufacturing and production, just to name a few. But speed doesn't automatically equal success. Or victory. There's a lot more to it. There's a process of preparation that often determines the outcome. Are you more concerned with how quickly you can achieve your goals? Or are you focused on the journey and the process? Oftentimes, it's the journey that makes the difference. No one's path is a straight one. It involves detours, wrong turns and missed exits. Restarts and backtracking. And it's on this journey that God molds us. He teaches us. He leads us. God uses our journey, not our achievements. Don't be concerned with getting there the fastest. Be concerned with walking with God on your journey. Enjoy His presence, His leading and His corrections. You'll get there in due time.

DAY 167

"I don't know why people like the home run so much. A home run is over as soon as it starts. The triple is the most exciting play of the game." George Foster

For they are like a breath of air; their days are like a passing shadow.

Psalms 144:4

Life goes by quickly. And the older we get, the faster it goes. We blink our eyes and our kids are grown. We blink our eyes and chapters are closed and seasons are done. It almost seems like it's over as soon as it starts. So how are you making your days count? How are you going to make today matter? Hopefully by starting your day with time spent with God. When you are in relationship with Him, your life takes on new meaning. You begin to understand that your time is limited. And most importantly, you understand that time doesn't belong to you. It belongs to God. And in His grace and mercy, He gives us more time each day. So use it wisely. Make it count. Make it about Him. Because it will be over before you know it!

DAY 168

"I don't put any foreign substances on the baseball. Everything I use is from the good old USA." George Frazier

The land must never be sold on a permanent basis, for the land belongs to me. You are only foreigners and tenant farmers working for me. Leviticus 25:23

Much like the Israelites, we are all still foreigners and tenant farmers. This isn't our home. It's only temporary housing. Our true home and destination is heaven. We are in this world, but as followers of Jesus Christ, we are not of this world. God placed you here for a reason and for a purpose. To tell others about the saving power of Jesus. To bring about the Kingdom of God. But it's not forever. We are only passing through. But while you are here, proclaim the Gospel to everyone. And live out the Gospel for everyone to see!

DAY 169

"I'm rich. What am I supposed to do, hide it?" Lou Whitaker

Teach those who are rich in this world not to be proud and not to trust in their money, which is so unreliable. Their trust should be in God, who richly gives us all we need for our enjoyment. Tell them to use their money to do good.

1 Timothy 6:17-18

If you are financially blessed, do not be ashamed. Chances are, you worked hard for your money. Sacrifices were likely made along the way to help you achieve financial security. So don't hide it. But don't brag about it either. Instead, use it to do good. Help others. Support your family with it. Glorify God with it. But don't flaunt it. And don't place your trust in it. Instead, place your trust in God. Thank Him for your riches and for providing for all your needs. And then use it to impact the lives of those around you. Use your blessings today to be a blessing!

DAY 170

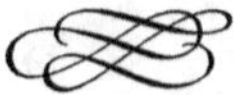

"I couldn't see well enough to play when I was a boy so they gave me a special job. They made me an umpire." Harry Truman

If we claim we have no sin, we are only fooling ourselves and not living in the truth. 1 John 1:8

How good is your vision? Do you see the shortcomings of others easily but struggle to see your own shortcomings? If so, it's time to get your eyes checked again! Seeing the mistakes of others is easy. But seeing your own is painful. It's difficult. And it can be disheartening. But the truth is, no one is perfect. Not even close. The sooner you acknowledge your mistakes, sins and imperfections, the sooner you will walk in the light of God's truth. And the closer you grow to God. We can't fix ourselves. But God can. We can't save ourselves. But Jesus can. Take a look at yourself today. See your sin. Confess it. And let the blood of Jesus make you clean!

DAY 171

"I'm the straw that stirs the drink." Reggie Jackson

An angry person starts fights; a hot-tempered person commits all kinds of sin. Proverbs 29:22

Are you an instigator? An agitator? A pot-stirrer? If so, it's time to change your ways. Stirring up trouble will always get you in trouble. It destroys peace. It creates chaos. And it serves no purpose. You were created to live in harmony and peace with one another. And with God. Hurt people hurt people. And misery loves company. Living close to God requires living in peace. When you live in anger, it results in sinful behaviors - like intentionally hurting others. So today, ask God to give you peace so you can live in peace with everyone. You'll be thankful. And so will those around you!

DAY 172

"I led the league in 'go get 'em next time." Bob Uecker

Wise words bring many benefits, and hard work brings rewards.

Proverbs 12:24

"Go get 'em next time." Intended to bring comfort and encouragement, these words are only spoken after a failed attempt and when we need it most. How do you respond to others' failures? Are you encouraging and supportive? Do you approach them with gentle reassurance or do you leave them to figure it out on their own? A pat on the back is sometimes all that's needed to lift someone's spirits. And an "I believe in you" can go a long way in restoring their confidence. Choose your words wisely. Be supportive and be encouraging. The same way God is with you!

DAY 173

"I am the best in baseball." Reggie Jackson

Then his disciples began arguing about who was the greatest. Luke 9:48

Confidence is key when it comes to success. Believing in your God given talents and abilities will take you far in life. But you must be mindful that your confidence doesn't turn into arrogance and begin thinking that you're the greatest or the best. That sort of mindset serves no purpose. Especially in the Kingdom of God. In the Kingdom, humility is key. Never thinking too highly of ourselves. Never thinking we're better than everyone. Jesus teaches that in order to be seen as the greatest, you must view yourself as the least and be willing to put others first. You must be willing to remove your ego and welcome Him into your hearts. In doing so, you will be viewed as the greatest in the Kingdom of God!

DAY 174

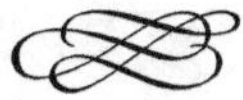

"Don't pray when it rains if you don't pray when the sun shines." Satchel Paige

Always be joyful. Never stop praying. 1 Thessalonians 5:16-17

God is always in control. No matter the circumstances. Whether it's raining or the sun is shining, He's always in control. Whether you are in a valley or on a mountaintop, God is still the same. And He uses these times to help you grow closer to Him. It's not easy because life can be challenging. But the Holy Spirit lives in you, so that you may praise Him and rejoice always. In the good times, and the bad, God is always in control. Praise Him today and every day, regardless of your circumstances!

DAY 175

"It actually giggles at you as it goes by." Rick Monday on Phil Niekro's knuckleball

He will once again fill your mouth with laughter and your lips with shouts of joy. Job 8:21

Have you ever felt like the world is laughing at you because of your problems? Friends, family, strangers? Even the thing that is causing the difficulties in your life is laughing at you? It seems as though the pain, the shame and the embarrassment will never end. But it will. This season is only temporary. God's promises are forever. He is with you. He is guiding you through your challenges. And as He does, your mouth will be filled with laughter. And shouts of joy will flow from your lips. You will be the one laughing because of the great faithfulness of God!

DAY 176

"The key to winning baseball games is pitching, fundamentals and three run homers." Earl Weaver

Study this Book of Instruction continually. Meditate on it day and night so you will be sure to obey everything written in it. Only then will you prosper and succeed in all you do. Joshua 1:8

Do you want to be successful? Do you want to prosper in everything you do? Of course you do! No one wants to fail. No one wants to be viewed as unsuccessful. So how do you succeed and become prosperous in life? It's simple. By studying the Bible daily. Day and night. Meditating on God's Word. Not just reading it but absorbing it. Living it. Being obedient to it. Consume the Bible and let it consume you. Become obsessed with His Word. The answers to your problems are found in the Bible. The keys to victory for your life are found in the Bible. Study it. And be obedient. Amen.

DAY 177

"All ball players should quit when it starts to feel like the baselines run uphill."

Babe Ruth

For the Lord your God is going with you! He will fight for you against your enemies, and he will give you victory! Deuteronomy 20:4

Quitting when the baselines feel like running uphill is probably a good idea for baseball players. But quitting when life feels like an uphill battle is never a good idea. Challenges arise. Difficulties appear. Sometimes speed bumps feel like immovable mountains. But you never face them alone. God is always with you. He is your protector. Hewatches over you. No matter what you're facing, you will never face it alone. And because of this, victory is only a prayer away. So turn to God and allow Him to fight your battles. Not just today, but everyday!

DAY 178

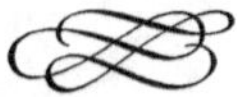

"Everywhere I go, people love me, so I'm just blessed."
Manny Ramirez

Wherever you go and whatever you do, you will be blessed. Deuteronomy 28:6

We all want to be liked. And we all want to be blessed. Being liked involves receiving approval from others. Being blessed is receiving approval from God. Which one is more important to you? Blessed or liked? Being liked often involves pleasing people. Being blessed always involves pleasing God. And nothing pleases God more than obedience. Studying His Word. Living out His Word. Keeping His commandments. Being liked is easy - just do what people want. But being blessed is more difficult because it requires obedience. And obedience requires discipline and commitment. When given the opportunity today to be blessed or liked, choose blessed. It's so much better! Obey God and His blessings will follow!

DAY 179

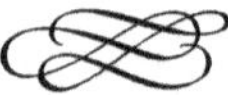

"There has always been a saying in baseball that you can't make a hitter, but I think you can improve a hitter. More than you can improve a fielder."

Ted Williams

Throw off your old sinful nature and your former way of life, which is corrupted by lust and deception. Instead, let the Spirit renew your thoughts and attitudes. Put on your new nature, created to be like God - truly righteous and holy. Ephesians 4:22-24

By definition, improve means to "make or become better." Room for growth. And improving is something we can all do, whether we like to admit it or not. We can improve our physical health through exercise and working out. We can improve our diet by changing our eating habits. And we can change our attitudes and thoughts through a relationship with Jesus Christ. No matter how hard you try to change and improve, it's impossible unless your life is surrendered to the one who gave His life for you. Becoming more holy and righteous is a daily improvement we should all strive for. But without God, our efforts are useless. So today, focus on your relationship with Christ and the improvements will come naturally!

DAY 180

"It's the mathematical potential for a game to last forever."
Bill Vaughn

The grass withers and the flowers fade, but the word of our God stands forever. Isaiah 40:8

Although mathematically possible, baseball games do not last forever. They eventually come to an end. In fact, everything does. Seasons. Relationships. Vacations. Life. "But the word of God stands forever." Always relevant. Always timely. And always true. Where do you go when seeking counsel? Where do you place your trust? Where do you find hope? In the Word of God. It never fades. And it never fails. No matter what you're facing, the answer will be found in God's Word. So today, commit yourself to His Word. It doesn't change. But it will change you!

DAY 181

"I never feel more at home than at a ballgame." Robert Frost

For we know that when this earthly tent we live in is taken down, we will have a house in heaven, an eternal body made for us by God himself and not by human hands. 2 Corinthians 5:1

Tents are temporary dwellings. Designed to minimally protect those dwelling in them from the weather and elements, they are not designed to be lived in forever. And neither are our bodies. Our bodies are also temporary and designed to protect that which dwells inside - the Spirit of God. Although God's Spirit is indestructible, the dwelling that protects it (our bodies) can be damaged. Scrapes, bruises, burns and cuts. Broken bones and broken feelings. Our bodies endure a lot. But waiting for you in heaven is a dwelling that will last forever. A new home and a new heavenly body created by God. Better than anything created on earth.

DAY 182

"To me, baseball was a passion to the point of obsession."
Brooks Robinson

You must not covet your neighbor's house. You must not covet your neighbor's wife, male or female servant, ox or donkey, or anything else that belongs to your neighbor. Exodus 20:17

Is there something in your life that you are obsessed with? Money? Success? Fame? Another person? When we are obsessed with something, it consumes us. It's all we think about. It controls everything about our lives. Our thoughts. Our actions. Which is why obsession is so dangerous. God warns us about obsession in The Ten Commandments. To covet is not just to want or admire. It is to become obsessed with. There is only one thing you should ever become obsessed with and controlled by. Your relationship with God. Be consumed by God's Word. Be obsessed with growing in relationship with Him. Commit yourself to Him and Him alone. It's the only safe obsession you'll ever have!

DAY 183

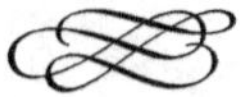

"More mistakes are made hitting than in any other part of the game." Ted Williams

Each time he said, "My grace is all you need. My power works best in weakness." So now I am glad to boast about my weaknesses, so that the power of Christ can work through me. 2 Corinthians 12:9

Our lives are filled with mistakes. Accidents. Should've, could've and would've. Missteps and misspoken words. But it's in these moments that you learn and grow. And most importantly, it's when you see the power of God's grace and mercy. In our weaknesses, we are made strong. In our mistakes, we are made perfect. In our shame, we are made whole. All because of God's love for us. We're all going to make mistakes. None of us are perfect. But your mistakes don't define you. God's grace and love define you. Praise be to God!

DAY 184

"The great thing about baseball is that there's a crisis every day." Gabe Paul

The Lord hears his people when they call to him for help. He rescues them from all their troubles. Psalms 34:17

Have you ever started talking to someone only to realize that they had walked out of the room and didn't hear a word you said? Or better yet, told a story to someone who was actually in the room and have them reply, "Were you talking to me?" Luckily for us, that's never the case with God. He always hears you. No matter what you're facing, what we're dealing with or the circumstances you find yourself in, God is always listening. He hears you when you cry out. He hears your pleas for help. All you have to do is ask. Have you called on God recently in the midst of your crisis? He's waiting to hear from you!

DAY 185

"In baseball, there's always tomorrow." Ryne Sandberg

Great is his faithfulness; his mercies begin afresh each morning.

Lamentations 3:23

Tomorrow. The day of hope. Hope for improvement. Hope for change in circumstances. Hope for a better day. A fresh start is sometimes all we need. Just like God's mercies. They "begin afresh" each day. It's been said that "all good things must come to an end." God's mercy isn't one of those things. It never runs out. It never comes to an end. Because He loves you. Today. And tomorrow.

DAY 186

"The key to being a good manager is keeping the people who hate me away from those who are still undecided." Casey Stengel

A church leader is a manager of God's household, so he must live a blameless life. Titus 1:7

Being a good manager is never easy. It always comes with great responsibility. You are responsible for the scheduling, finances and managing the personalities of your employees. You're also responsible for managing yourself. Conducting yourself in a manner that is consistent with the company's values, both professionally and personally. It's no different in the church. Whether you are a pastor, an elder or a volunteer, you are part of God's management team. And your actions matter - at church and most importantly, at home. Are you leading a life that is consistent with the Word of God? Does your life reflect the light of Christ as you walk with Him? Ask God today for his guidance in all of your management responsibilities. The ones you lead will reap the benefits and so will you!

DAY 187

"He looks like a greyhound but he runs like a bus." George Brett on teammate Jamie Quirk

Beware of false prophets who come disguised as harmless sheep but are really vicious wolves. Matthew 7:15

Deception is a tool of the devil. It's used by those looking to get ahead in dishonest ways. It's used to take advantage of others. And it's used to cover up personal insecurities. Deception leaves a wake of broken trust and betrayal along its path. And Jesus warns us about those who are deceitful, both in their personal lives and in the church. They present themselves as one way, but deep down they are evil and looking to take advantage of the people around them. Deceitful people can be identified by the fruit they produce. Good people produce good fruit. Ask God to help you discern the messages and the motives of those you interact with today. And be on the lookout for bad fruit!

DAY 188

"I feel greatly honored to have a ballpark named after me, especially since I've been thrown out of so many." Casey Stengel

Respect everyone, and love the family of God. Fear God, and respect the king.

1 Peter 2:17

Respect. Always desired, but often hard to give. Especially to those we disagree with or believe they don't deserve it. So how do we know how and who to respect? The answer is simple: "Respect everyone." As a follower of Christ, you are instructed to respect all people. Even the ones who don't deserve it. Even the ones who haven't earned it. We do this because of our obedience to Christ and our love for Him and the Kingdom of God. Period.

DAY 189

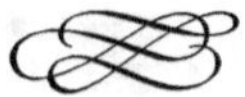

"There is an old saying that money can't buy happiness. If it could, I would buy myself four hits every game." Pete Rose

But Peter replied, "May your money be destroyed with you for thinking God's gift can be bought!" Acts 8:20

Money can't buy happiness or love. And as Simon found out, money can't buy God's power either. After seeing many miracles being performed by the disciples, Simon saw a "business" opportunity. He wanted to purchase this gift and use it to make a profit for himself, which elicited this harsh response from Peter. The Holy Spirit cannot be purchased and neither can love or happiness. They all come from having a deeply intimate and personal relationship with Jesus Christ. True joy comes from knowing and trusting God, as does love. And the Holy Spirit dwells inside us when we make Jesus Christ Lord of our lives. Instead of investing your money, invest your heart and your time into a loving relationship with God. Then you will prosper!

DAY 190

"Here I am a baseball superstar, falling into the pits, having everybody write you off and then having God say "I'm going to use your mess for a message." How beautiful is that?" Daryl Strawberry

Publish his glorious deeds among the nations. Tell everyone about the amazing things he has done. Psalms 96:3

God specializes in turning our mess into a message. Turning our low points into teaching points. Turning our goof ups to glory. And when He does, we are called to share our story. To proclaim His redeeming goodness to the world. Whether you realize it or not, your faith story can and will impact the lives of others - possibly for generations to come. Sharing your story may seem nerve racking or intimidating or pushy, but you experienced it for a reason. Not only to strengthen your faith, but to help others. Ask God to give you an opportunity to share your mess turned message with someone today. You need to tell it. And someone needs to hear it!

DAY 191

"One of the nicest satisfactions you can have is to be able to give something back to your parents when they've given so much." Dwight Gooden

Honor your father and mother. Exodus 20:12

Parents often sacrifice a lot for their children. Time, sleep, going without themselves so their kids can have. The list is endless. As children, we are called to honor, respect and obey them. Not only because we are instructed to, but because we want to. Our parents don't ask for anything in return. They sacrifice because of their love for their children. So be respectful of them. Spend time with them. Pray for them. Honoring your parents doesn't mean buying them a house or a car. It means treating them with respect in all that you do. Ask God to help you if this is something you struggle with. And if you're already honoring them in your life, keep it up. Because your kids are watching!

DAY 192

"Let me get this straight. The owners are about to shut down baseball when it's more prosperous than it's ever been and the players are the ones who have to get their urine tested?"
Ron Darling

You intended to harm me but God intended it all for good. He brought me to this position so I could save the lives of many people. Genesis 50:20

Sometimes life doesn't make sense. It leaves us shaking our fists asking God how and why. Job losses. Cancer diagnoses. Accidents. Death. "God, how could you let this happen? Why did you let this happen?" But in the midst of it all, God is still with you. He's still in control. And what the enemy intended for evil, God can use for good - if you let Him. So when the events of your life don't make sense, talk to God. Trust Him. And allow Him to lead you through it. No matter how confusing and difficult it may be. Today and always.

DAY 193

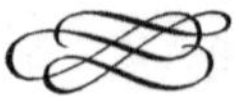

"What you lack in talent can be made up with desire, hustle and giving 110% all the time." Don Zimmer

And so, dear brothers and sisters, I plead with you to give your bodies to God because of all he has done for you. Let them be a living and holy sacrifice - the kind he will find acceptable. This is truly the way to worship him. Romans 12:1

Giving 110% is not humanly possible. All you can give is 100% of what you have. And that is your body, which includes your heart, mind and soul. God has given us everything, including salvation through the death of His Son on the cross. So for you to give less than everything in return is not right. God deserves our all. Are you giving it to Him? Or are you holding something back? If so, it's time to make a change. Give your bodies to God. Dedicate your life to him. It's worth the sacrifice. Amen.

DAY 194

"I'll never take for granted the opportunity to put on a Dodgers uniform."

Clayton Kershaw

Let all that I am praise the Lord; may I never forget the good things he does for me. Psalms 103:2

Every day is an opportunity to praise and worship God. With your words and with your actions. We are blessed because of God's goodness. Each day is a gift. Are you approaching it with a grateful heart or do you take it for granted? Does your heart reflect God's love and mercy to others? If not, ask God to help you change today. Tomorrow isn't promised. Be grateful for this day. And for the opportunity to praise Him. Always.

DAY 195

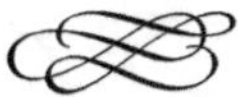

"Christianity is called a spiritual walk. It's not a run and it's not a jog. It's a walk you do from day to day and that makes you stable." Orel Hershiser

Your word is a lamp to guide my feet and a light for my path. Psalms 119:105

A spiritual walk, not a spiritual sprint. It often leads us along a path that can sometimes seem dark and scary. But it doesn't have to be. Because you have a lamp and a guide for your daily walk. God's Word. When you are led by His Word, nothing you face is too challenging. Nothing is impossible. Because God is leading you through the good times and the bad. Through the smooth times and the difficult. Are you walking with God each day? Does His word guide your steps and light your path? Make the decision to follow wherever He leads you today. And tomorrow. And the next day…

DAY 196

"I don't think some athletes understand how big it is to be an athlete, what they can do with just a simple gesture of shaking a kid's hand. It can make a fan's day. It can make a fan's life." Matt Kemp

Love each other with genuine affection, and take delight in honoring each other. Romans 12:10

Never underestimate the power of your words and your actions on the lives of others. What seems small and insignificant to you can make a huge impact on the life of someone else. And you may not even realize it. A hug. A handshake. A kind greeting. We never know what other people are going through. Paul's words are clear. Love one another. Honor each other. Be genuine and a difference maker. Starting today!

DAY 197

"Has he (Rickey Henderson) ever been here (Spring Training) the first day? You have to say Rickey's consistent. That's what you want in a ball player - consistency."

Don Mattingly

Remain in me, and I will remain in you. For a branch cannot produce fruit if it is severed from the vine, and you cannot be fruitful unless you remain in me. John 15:4

How consistent is your relationship with God? Do you only visit with him once a week, maybe on Sunday? Do you pop in for a quick visit every now and then when you need something? Or do you spend time with Him throughout your day, every day? Hopefully the answer is every day! Consistency is important in developing relationships in our personal lives and it's no different with our spiritual lives. The only way to grow closer to God is by spending time with Him. In prayer. In His Word. In silent meditation. In all areas of our lives, consistency is key. Especially in your relationship with God.

DAY 198

"You've got to be very careful if you don't know where you are going, because you might not get there." Yogi Berra

And you know the way to where I am going. "No, we don't know, Lord," Thomas said. "We have no idea where you are going, so how can we know the way?" John 14:4-5

Getting lost is easy to do, especially if you don't know where you are going. Even with directions, getting lost can sometimes happen. Do you know where you are going? Are you traveling on the path of righteousness that leads to eternal life with the Father? Or is there some doubt in your mind on where you are heading? There is only one way to eternal life. And that is through a relationship with Jesus Christ. He is the Way. If you haven't already done it, ask Jesus to come into your heart. Enter into a relationship with Him so you may know God the Father. And there will be no doubt as to where you are going!

DAY 199

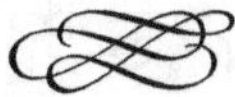

"Always go to other people's funerals, otherwise they won't come to yours."

Yogi Berra

So whatever you wish that others would do to you, do also to them, for this is the Law and the Prophets. Matthew 7:12

The Golden Rule. Treat others the way you want to be treated. Do you want to be forgiven for your mistakes? Forgive others. Do you want to be helped and counseled when going through difficult times? Help and counsel others. Do you want to be blessed in life? Be a blessing to others. Jesus's words are quite simple and direct. Wise words to live by, spoken by our Savior. Follow them, starting today!

DAY 200

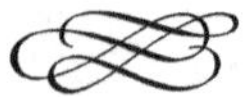

"Where would I be without baseball? Who am I without baseball?" Bob Uecker

For we are God's masterpiece. He has created us anew in Christ Jesus, so we can do the good things he planned for us long ago. Ephesians 2:10

Many people wrestle with their identity. And many others lose it. In relationships. In jobs. In life's struggles. Who are you? The answer is simple. You are God's masterpiece. You were created to do and accomplish great things. Things orchestrated by God and designed especially for you. You may be a great athlete. But that will one day come to an end. You may be a great teacher, coach or businessman. One day you will retire but you will never stop being God's masterpiece. He created you for a purpose. You have an assignment. And it starts today. Be the Light this world desperately needs. Give God thanks and ask Him to use you for the glory of His Kingdom.

DAY 201

"In baseball, you don't know nothing." Yogi Berra

He will come with his mighty angels, in flaming fire, bringing judgment on those who don't know God and on those who refuse to obey the Good News of our Lord Jesus. 2 Thessalonians 1:7b-8

Oftentimes in life, we find that ignorance is bliss. Sometimes it's just better not knowing. Sometimes life is simpler that way. But it's not that way with God. Life is always better knowing Him. Having a relationship with Jesus. When you come face to face with God once your time on earth is done, ignorance will not be bliss. Far from it. Do you know God? Or do you just know of Him? Do you follow the teachings of Christ or just the ones that are easy to follow? God has claimed you as His child. Do you claim Him as your Heavenly Father? Knowing of God isn't good enough. Know Him intimately. Proclaim Him loudly. Follow the teachings of Christ daily. Your future depends on it.

DAY 202

"You never know what's going to happen...And that's the fun of it! That's what baseball is all about!" Keiichi Arawi

Don't brag about tomorrow, since you don't know what the day will bring.

Proverbs 27:1

Life is full of uncertainties. And our lives are no different. We are only promised today. We are only promised this moment. Don't waste it. Don't take it for granted. Tomorrow may bring job loss, bad news from the doctor or even death. Your life can change drastically tomorrow, or even in the coming hours. Treat this moment like the gift it is. Who should you love today? Who should you forgive today? Who should you comfort today? And most importantly, how can you glorify God today? He has given you this day, this moment. Praise Him. Glorify and praise Him. Today and always.

DAY 203

"If there are any curses left in baseball, they are all on the north side of Chicago." Tucker Elliot

But Christ has rescued us from the curse pronounced by the law. When he was hung on the cross, he took upon himself the curse for our wrongdoing. For it is written in the Scriptures, "Cursed is everyone who is hung on a tree." Galatians 3:13

According to The Law, we are all cursed because of our sin and cannot redeem ourselves. Redemption only comes through the blood of Jesus. He became our curse and removed it from our lives. Forgiveness and righteousness are ours because Christ was hung on the cross. Our curse could not be lifted, only transferred. Christ died for your sins. Does your life reflect the gratefulness we owe Him? Do you honor Him with your words, actions and thoughts? Do you forgive others like you've been forgiven? You should. He lifted the curse so that you can live for Him.

"Fenway is the essence of baseball." Tom Seaver

But anyone who does not love does not know God, for God is love. 1 John 4:8

The very essence of God is love. It is not contingent upon our behavior. It doesn't fluctuate from day to day. His love is unconditional. He loves us. Always and forever. Do you love others, as God first loved you? Not just friends and family, but everyone. Even the unlovable. Do you love them too? When our lives are fully devoted to God and guided by the Holy Spirit, we reflect His love in all we do, to everyone we meet. Do you love God? If so, let your love for Him be shown by your love for others! Then the world will know God's love firsthand!

<h1 style="text-align:center">DAY 205</h1>

"Baseball, it is said, is only a game. True. And the Grand Canyon is only a hole in Arizona. Not all holes, or games, are created equal." George Will

Then Peter replied, "I see very clearly that God shows no favoritism."

Acts 10:34

Each one of us were given different gifts and talents to be used in different ways for the Kingdom of God. Our gifts and talents are what makes us unique. But God loves us equally. He does not show partiality or favoritism. We are all precious to Him. Regardless of our social status. Regardless of our birthplace. He sees us all the same. We are all His children. This was a hard lesson for many Jews to understand. That Gentiles could receive the same in-dwelling of the Holy Spirit as them and therefore be accepted into God's Kingdom just as they had been. But it is true. The Kingdom of God is for everyone. No matter where you were born. Or where you were raised. We are all God's children, equal in His eyes.

DAY 206

"There are three things you can do in a baseball game. You can win, you can lose or it can rain." Casey Stengel

Don't you realize that in a race everyone runs but only one person gets the prize? So run to win! 1 Corinthians 9:24

Winning is fun. It makes us feel good. We win games. We win prizes. We win recognition. Luckily for us, we don't have to worry about winning our salvation. In God's grace, we receive it when we accept Jesus as Lord of our life. But we still run the race. And not half heartedly. We give our all. For God's Kingdom and for His glory. Our prize is in Heaven. So no matter where you are running your race, in sickness, at work or in the community, give it your best. Run to win. A heavenly prize awaits you!

<h1 style="text-align:center">DAY 207</h1>

"Baseball is 90% mental. The other half is physical." Yogi Berra

Now may the God of peace make you holy in every way, and may your whole spirit and soul and body be kept blameless until our Lord Jesus Christ comes again. 1 Thessalonians 5:23

Yogi's math may be off, but his message is clear. Baseball requires a 100% commitment that involves both body and mind. And so does your relationship with God. When you are fully devoted to serving, loving and knowing Him, He will make you "holy in every way." Your thoughts, your actions, and your intentions. Everything will be made holy. But you must also be devoted to keeping your whole spirit, soul and body blameless until his glorious return. Not just sometimes. Not just part of your life. All of it. All the time. Wholly devoted. Amen.

DAY 208

"Baseball is a game of inches." Branch Rickey

So you will see the land from a distance, but you may not enter the land I am giving to the people of Israel. Deuteronomy 32:51

God's will for your life. How closely are you following His plan? Are you in step with it? Or are you miles away, doing your own thing? Or are you close but no cigar? Just inches away? Moses was close. Really close. And he was close to the Promised Land too. He could see the land flowing with milk and honey. But he never would enter the land. His disobedience and treatment of God prevented him from one day entering it. Close wasn't good enough. Being in the vicinity didn't work. Doesn't work in baseball. And not in your walk with God either. Starting today, faithfully commit your words, your actions and your heart to God. Don't settle for inches away, only seeing His goodness from a distance. Walk hand in hand. Daily. And experience God's promises first hand!

"A no-hitter is a freaky thing. Most of the greatest pitchers never pitched one. It's a combination of a lot of little accidents." Duane Decker

You can make many plans, but the Lord's purpose will prevail. Proverbs 19:21

There are no accidents with God. The family you were born into. Your job. Broken relationships. Where you are in life. Even if it's the result of an accident. It wasn't an accident to God. His plan is perfect. And so are His ways and His timing. No matter where you are in life or what you are facing, God is using it for your good. And for His Glory. Amen.

"Athletes are born winners, they're not born losers, and the sooner you understand this, the faster you can take on a winning attitude and become successful in life." Charles R. Sledge, Jr.

But those who trust in the Lord will find new strength. They will soar high on wings like eagles. They will run and not grow weary. They will walk and not faint. Isaiah 40:31

Our strength comes from God. He gives us strength. And He is our strength. Are you carrying heavy burdens? Give them to God. He's strong enough to carry them for you. Are you currently facing challenges in your life? Turn to God and ask Him for strength. Are you feeling weak? God will strengthen you. No amount of time in a weight room, no amount of time running on a track will ever compare to the strength that God gives you. He is strong enough to carry your worries. And He is strong enough to carry you through whatever you are facing. All you have to do is ask!

DAY 211

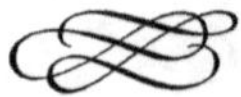

"A baseball player spends a good piece of his life gripping a baseball, and in the end, it turns out that it was the other way around all the time." Jim Bouton

For even the Son of Man came not to be served but to serve others and to give his life as a ransom for many. Mark 10:45

Too many times, we get our assignments in life wrong. From our perspectives to our missions, we miss the point. Our current culture teaches the attitude of "what have you done for me lately." And "what can I get from you" or "what's in it for me." But our culture is teaching us wrong. Actually it's the other way around! Jesus's life teaches us the opposite. Jesus didn't come to be served, but to serve. To love unconditionally, expecting nothing in return. Love and service. Pillars of our faith. Are you practicing what Jesus preached?

DAY 212

"There's no crying in baseball!" Tom Hanks (A League Of Their Own)

You keep track of all my sorrows. You have collected all my tears in your bottle. You have recorded each one in your book. Psalms 56:8

There may not be any crying in baseball, but there's crying in life. Sadness. Hurt feelings. Loss. Makes us feel like crying. Sometimes we do. And it's okay. Because God sees you. He hears you. And He hurts with you and for you. Your tears matter to God. Not only does He bottle our tears, He wipes them away too. With gentleness and love. So cry. Because you are never alone. God sees you. And He's with you. Always.

DAY 213

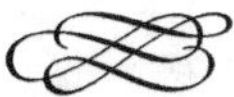

"No one has come up with a substitute for hard work." Ted Williams

And hardworking farmers should be the first to enjoy the fruit of their labor.

2 Timothy 2:6

Farming is hard work and therefore, farmers have to be hard workers. It requires sweat, long hours, devotion and precise timing. But regardless of their efforts, it is God who is ultimately responsible for the harvest. And it's no different with our lives as followers of Christ. Our faith walk also requires timing, devotion and hard work. And just like farmers, our harvest is dependent upon God. So whether it's on the field, at your job or in the classroom, work hard. Because there is no substitute for hard work. And trust God for the harvest!

DAY 214

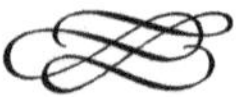

"Don't ever let the pressure exceed the pleasure." Joe Maddon

When the cares of my heart are many, your consolations cheer my soul.

Psalms 94:19

Oftentimes our lives are filled with pressure and expectations. Sometimes they're unrealistic. In the classroom, at work, on the field and at home. How will we ever live up to the expectations? How will we overcome the pressures of life? If only we could tell God how things need to go! Then it would be okay! But God sees all and knows all. And He's with us through it all. And that is where we find our comfort and peace. Knowing that God has already worked things out for our good. Enjoy the journey. Enjoy the challenge. God's got this! And He's got you too!

DAY 215

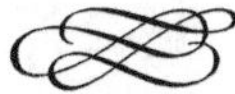

"Bob Gibson is the luckiest pitcher I ever saw. He always pitches when the other team doesn't score any runs." Tim McCarver

If you openly declare that Jesus is Lord and believe in your heart that God raised him from the dead, you will be saved. Romans 10:9

Luck is what happens when preparation meets hard work (Seneca). Just like we often create our own path in life, sometimes we create our own luck too. Our choices and preparation, or lack thereof, go a long way in determining our successes and our failures. Everyone is faced with different choices in life. But there is one choice that is the same for all of us. Will you accept Jesus as the Lord of your life? And will you confess it openly for all to know? When you do this, you will be saved. And eternal life will be yours!

DAY 216

"We know we're better than this, but we can't prove it." Tony Gwynn

Work hard so you can present yourself to God and receive his approval. Be a good worker, one who does not need to be ashamed and who correctly explains the word of truth. 2 Timothy 2:15

Too many times, feelings of self doubt and inadequacy lead us to feeling as though we need to prove ourselves. To our coaches, our teammates, our friends and even our families. To show that we belong. That we're good enough. That we are enough. And this can be exhausting and saddening. Because to some, no matter what you do or say, it will never be good enough. But there is only one that you should try to prove yourself to. God. And you do this by ensuring that your words and your actions are aligned with one another. That we speak love and act in love. Speak truth and live in truth. Because God's approval is the only one that matters!

"It ain't like football. You can't make up no trick plays." Yogi Berra

These people are false apostles. They are deceitful workers who disguise themselves as apostles of Christ. 2 Corinthians 11:13

Trick plays are part of sports. And unfortunately, they are part of the world we live in. Using deception and deceit to gain an advantage. Paul faced and confronted them in Corinth and we still face them today. Especially when teaching God's Word. False teachings. Skewed truths. Selfish motives. Be careful of the messengers. They may sound genuine, but are far from it. Self proclaimed servants of God but actually servants of Satan. Ask God to help you discern His Word. And the motivation of the one delivering it!

DAY 218

"I think I throw the ball as hard as anyone. The ball just doesn't get there as fast." Eddie Bane

Because of the privilege and authority God has given me, I give each of you this warning: Don't think you are better than you really are. Be honest in your evaluation of yourselves, measuring yourselves by the faith God has given us. Romans 12:3

No one knows you better than you. No one. Because of this, you must be honest with yourself about your overall health, progress and growth. How is your physical, mental and emotional health? And most importantly, how is your spiritual health? Are you spending time with God daily? Reading His Word? Talking to Him in prayer? Reflecting His love to others? In other words, is your walk with Christ where you think it should be? If so, keep it up! But if it needs improvement, be honest with yourself. And take the necessary steps to grow in your relationship with Christ!

DAY 219

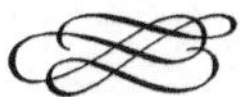

"What are we out at the park for, except to win?" Leo Durocher

Don't you realize that in a race everyone runs, but only one person gets the prize? So run to win! 1 Corinthians 9:24

Do you live each day with purpose? With real intent? Or do you just drift through your day and your life with no real direction? Drifting allows the world to lead you. Purpose allows God to lead you. When you live your life with purpose, God becomes the focal point of your life. Following His lead. Sensing His presence. Responding to His call. You were created for a purpose. God placed a call on your life. Follow His call and His direction. Live this day and everyday with purpose by following Him on purpose!

"I come to win." Leo Durocher

For I can do everything through Christ, who gives me strength."

Philippians 4:13

It's true. God provides us with strength. Strength to endure. Strength to overcome. Strength to stand strong in the face of adversity. And because of this, we can do all things because of the One who gives us our strength. God. No matter what you're facing, no matter where you are in life, God gives you the ability to overcome. To rise. And in doing so, the source of your strength will be glorified. God is our provider. Of our talents, our blessings and most importantly, our strength. So lean on Him, depend on Him. Today and forever.

<h1 style="text-align:center">DAY 221</h1>

"There isn't enough mustard in the whole world to cover that hot dog."

Darold Knowles on Reggie Jackson

For those who exalt themselves will be humbled, and those who humble themselves will be exalted. Luke 14:11

Humility is a painful lesson to learn. It can be embarrassing and it can be painful. Jesus teaches us to remain humble in all that we do. In all facets of our lives. Being humble means we are teachable and coachable. That we can be corrected and redirected. It means that we know that we don't have all the answers and understand our ways and our thoughts aren't always right. And when we realize this, God can speak to us. He can correct you and lead you on His path. Remaining humble allows you to grow closer to God. And that is the goal for today and every day!

DAY 222

"When I looked at the 3rd base coach, he turned his back on me." Bob Uecker

Never pay back evil with more evil. Do things in such a way that everyone can see that you are honorable. Romans 12:17

Everyone has been hurt by someone. Betrayed. Lied to. Forgotten. Ignored. It hurts because it's painful when someone we considered a friend or a loved one seemingly turns their back on us. Especially when we needed them the most. So how do you respond in times like these? Do you repay evil with evil, wrong with wrong? Our verse today teaches us to respond in a way that is honorable. In a way that reflects the holiness and mercy of God. Although man may turn his back on you, God never will. He will always be there, no matter your circumstances. So when others turn their back on you, respond with mercy. And turn to God. He's the only One who will always be there in your time of need.

<h1 style="text-align:center">DAY 223</h1>

"Please God, let me hit one. I'll tell everyone that you did it."
Reggie Jackson

God did it for us. Out of sheer generosity, he put us in right standing with himself. Romans 3:24

God did it. All of it. Our blessings? God did it. Getting us through those times we thought would cripple us? God did it. Forgiving our sins? God did it. Restoring us to where He desires us to be? Yep, God did that too. He did it all. Out of mercy and love and a desire to have you in relationship with Him, He did it. So don't take credit for what God has done. And don't give the credit to someone else or credit it to luck. God did it. Give Him the credit and give Him your life. It's the only thing He ask for in return!

DAY 224

"I never questioned the integrity of an umpire. Their eyesight, yes." Leo Durocher

Open my eyes to see the wonderful truths in your instructions. Psalms 119:18

Umpires are often accused of being blind. But in many ways, we are too - spiritually blind. We fail to see the blessings in our own lives while constantly asking for more. We ask God to answer our prayers but often, His answer is right in front of us. And we try to study His Word without asking Him to replace our spiritual blindness with open eyes and an open heart. God's Word is wonderful! And we should study it daily. But before doing so, ask God to open your eyes so that you may see the beauty of His Word!

DAY 225

"God watches over drunks and 3rd basemen." Leo Durocher

The Lord keeps watch over you as you come and go, both now and forever.

Psalms 121:8

It's not an empty promise. It's an eternal promise. God watches over His people. All of them. And that includes you! No matter where you are or what you're doing, God is watching over you. So rest in His arms, knowing that He holds you safe. Today and forever!

DAY 226

"I never did say that you can't be a nice guy and win. I said that if I was playing 3rd base and my mother rounded 3rd with the winning run, I'd trip her up."

Leo Durocher

Instead, be kind to each other, tenderhearted, forgiving one another, just as God through Christ has forgiven you. Ephesians 4:32

Sometimes competitiveness gets in the way. Sometimes, it's our selfish desire to get even. Sometimes it's acting before thinking. There are a multitude of reasons why we don't always act in kindness. But they are never a justified excuse. No matter your circumstances, you are called to be kind. Paul makes it perfectly clear. Regardless of how others treat you or how you're feeling, always be kind. You may regret hurting someone's feelings but you'll never regret being kind!

DAY 227

"Your chances of winning, I've got to believe are really, really small when you score one run in eighteen innings." Clint Hurdle

But thanks be to God, who gives us the victory through our Lord Jesus Christ.

1 Corinthians 15:57

Victories are hard to come by. Whether on the field or in life, winning isn't easy. And it's definitely not guaranteed. No matter how much you prepare or how hard you work, the outcome doesn't always turn out the way you want. But there is one victory that is guaranteed. And it's because of the sacrifice of Jesus Christ. He paid the price for our sins. He took them to the cross. And when He rose from the grave, Jesus overcame death on our behalf. Because of Jesus, there's one victory that is promised. And that's a guarantee!

DAY 228

"Finish last in your league and they call you an idiot. Finish last in medical school and they call you doctor." Abe Lemons

So those who are last now will be first then, and those who are first will be last.

Matthew 20:16

Our competitive spirit drives our desire to finish first. To be the best. To win all the awards and trophies. So finishing last is never fun. But in the Kingdom of God, being last is admirable. Putting others first, putting God first and giving up everything for Him leads us to being first in God's eyes. God's Kingdom doesn't operate the way the world works. Striving to be the best doesn't guarantee your salvation. Nothing you do will earn it. Because salvation can't be earned. It's freely given through God's grace. So strive to finish first on the ball field, but remember it's okay to be last in the Kingdom. You'll still be viewed as great!

DAY 229

"There are peaks and valleys in this game. Right now we're in a valley - Death Valley." Kirby Puckett

Even though I walk through the valley of the shadow of death, I will fear no evil, for you are with me; your rod and your staff, they comfort me. Psalms 23:4

We all go through valleys in life. Those times when your circumstances and surroundings feel overwhelming. Those times when it feels like no matter how hard you try to dig your way out, you only dig a deeper hole. It can be scary and it can be frustrating. But remember, God is always with you. His presence is constant. And it's in Him that you find strength in the midst of the valleys. The valleys are only temporary, but God's peace and love are forever!

DAY 230

"Baseball is reassuring. It makes me feel like the world is not going to blow up." Sharon Olds.

He was fully convinced that God is able to do whatever he promises.

Romans 4:21

God is trustworthy. His promises are real. And even though it seems like the world around you is collapsing, His Word remains true. When the world presents limitations, God sees possibility. When the world shows you all the reasons you can't, God promises that He can. And He will. So trust Him. Trust what God has told you more than what the world is saying. His promises are real. Prepare to be amazed again and again and again.….!

DAY 231

"I'm glad I don't play anymore. I never could learn all of those handshakes."

Phil Rizzuto

Instruct the wise, and they will be even wiser. Teach the righteous, and they will learn even more. Proverbs 9:9

Today, humble yourself, open your heart and mind and be willing to learn. If you already consider yourself wise, learn something new and become wiser. Seek knowledge. Seek God's truth and accept correction. By doing so, you are already a wise man. Never stop learning. Never stop growing. So approach every day and every situation as an opportunity to become even wiser.

DAY 232

"Winning is the most important thing in my life after breathing. Breathing first, winning next." George Steinbrenner

Then the Lord God formed the man from the dust of the ground. He breathed the breath of life into the man's nostrils, and the man became a living person.

Genesis 2:7

The breath of life. It was breathed into the nostrils of Adam and it was breathed into you as well. God breathed life into each one of us. It wasn't a gust of wind that filled your lungs. It was His breath. So be grateful. Not only were you made in His image and His likeness, you were created by His breath. And you are still breathing it today. And every day. Thanks be to God!

DAY 233

"The best thing about baseball is that there is no homework."
Dan Quisenberry

And the people of Berea were more open minded than those in Thessalonica, and they listened eagerly to Paul's message. They searched the Scriptures day after day to see if Paul and Silas were teaching the truth. Acts 17:11

There's no homework in baseball and there's no homework for believers either. But there is required study. Lots of it. Much like the people of Berea, we are called to examine the Scriptures daily. In doing so, you learn more, you know more and ultimately, you grow more. You will grow in your understanding of the Word. And you will grow in your relationship with God. When you devote daily time to studying the Bible, the results are evident - to others, to you and to God. So get to studying! You'll be glad you did!

DAY 234

"The last words to the Star Spangled Banner? Play ball!" Author Unknown

But if you refuse to serve the Lord, then choose today whom you will serve. Would you prefer the gods your ancestors served beyond the Euphrates? Or will it be the gods of the Amorites in whose land you now live? But as for me and my family, we will serve the Lord. Joshua 24:15

Famous last words. Good or bad, they're the ones we all remember. Whether we speak them or hear them, they're often hard to forget. Joshua's last words in today's verse are an example. Some of the most famous and powerful words that Joshua ever spoke, the proclamation is impactful. Have you given Joshua's last words any thought? If you haven't, you should. Who will you serve? Who will your family serve? Will you be the one to lead them? Give these last words some thought and make the decision for yourself and your family! The time to decide is now!

DAY 235

"He has it in his body to be great." Casey Stengel

You will restore me to even greater honor and comfort me once again.

Psalms 71:21

Greatness. It's what we all strive for. Not to be decent. Or average. But great. No matter what we're doing, we want to be great. But you can't do it alone. You can't rely on yourself to achieve greatness. You can work hard and put in hours of practice. But greatness comes from God. He is the One who will lift you up. He is the One who restores. God is great. And in Him, and through Him, you too can become great. But it starts and ends with God. He is the source of greatness!

DAY 236

"Finding good players is easy. Getting them to play as a team is another story." Casey Stengel

Two people are better off than one, for they can help each other succeed. Ecclesiastes 4:9

Teamwork. Baseball wasn't created to be played alone. And neither was life. God places people around you to help. To assist. To pick you up when you stumble. In doing so, you are able to see the goodness of God. Whether it's a friend, a family member or a teammate, you are blessed to have them on this journey of life. When you reject them, you reject a gift from God. God often uses other people to lift you up, just as He uses you to lift others up as well. So work together. We are all teammates in God's Kingdom!

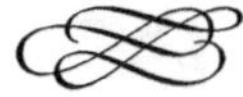

"You wouldn't have won if we'd beaten you." Yogi Berra

For every child of God defeats this evil world, and we achieve this victory through our faith. 1 John 4:5

Victory is sweet, oh so sweet! It's why we practice. It's why we study. We make sacrifices so when we take the field, we can be victorious. But victory is never certain and it's never guaranteed. But there is one victory that is certain and guaranteed. And it comes from our relationship with God Our Father. When we accept Jesus as Lord and Savior, we become a child of God. And in Him and through Him, our victory over this evil world is promised. You may endure hardships. You might experience loss. But the enemy will never prevail over you. So put your faith in Jesus. And victory over this world will be yours!

DAY 238

"The future ain't what it used to be." Yogi Berra

For I know the plans I have for you, says the Lord. They are plans for good and not for disaster, to give you a future and a hope. Jeremiah 29:11

Are you currently experiencing hardship in your life? A difficult time of pain and suffering? A time of confusion and uncertainty? Find comfort in today's verse. God promises us that our suffering will come to an end. Maybe not immediately. Maybe not today or tomorrow. Or even next week. But it will end. God promises that He has a plan for your life regardless of your current situation. His plan is full of love and grace. And in it, you will prosper. So today be filled with hope - God has a plan for you!

"If you're going to play at all, you're out to win. Baseball, board games, Jeopardy, I hate to lose." Derek Jeter

Those who love their life in this world will lose it. Those who care nothing for their life in this world will keep it for eternity. John 12:25

We all hate to lose. Regardless of the game, losing is never fun. Jesus speaks about losing. Losing our lives. And how to avoid it. When we love our lives and the ways of the world, then we are not living for God. We are living for ourselves and looking to appease the world. When you care more about your physical life than living for God and His Way, you are not living for eternal purposes. You must decide who you are living for - God or yourself. God put you here for a purpose. And to fulfill that purpose, you must be willing to lose your life and live for Him instead!

DAY 240

"When I knocked a guy down, there was no second part to the story." Bob Gibson

Fearing people is a dangerous trap, but trusting the Lord means safety.

Proverbs 29:25

Intimidation is part of baseball. Pitchers instilling fear in the batter. Batters instilling fear in the pitcher. It's a back and forth mind game designed to give one a mental advantage. Does it work? Maybe. But our verse today teaches us that we should never be intimidated by other people. Not in baseball, the classroom, the job site or anywhere. Instead, place your trust in the Lord. Allow Him to protect you. Allow Him to direct your thoughts and guide your steps. Intimidation leads to fear. Trusting God leads to safety. So today, choose safety. Choose God.

"Progress always involves risk. You can't steal second and keep your foot on first." Frederick B. Wilcox

"Yes, come," Jesus said. So Peter went over the side of the boat and walked on the water toward Jesus. Matthew 14:29

Peter took a risk. He could have sunk in the water. He could have drowned. But he didn't. He trusted Jesus and He followed Jesus. And Peter actually walked on the water, just as Jesus did. Is God calling you today? To follow Him and trust Him? Are you willing to go where He is leading you? It might seem scary. It might feel risky. But you can't steal second with your foot on first and you'll never walk on water if you stay in the boat. God is calling you. Follow Him. It's a "risk" worth taking!

DAY 242

"Just keep going. Everybody gets better if they keep at it." Ted Williams

One day Jesus told his disciples a story to show that they should always pray and never give up. Luke 18:1

Challenges can lead to frustration. But persistence leads to results. Are you at a point where you feel like giving up? Don't. Keep practicing. Keep trying. And keep praying. Ask God to lead and guide you. Ask Him to supply you with everything you need to stand tall in life's battles. And ask Him to strengthen you so you can face any issue that comes your way. Baseball is hard. Life is hard. But don't give up. Keep going. Lean on God and be persistent. You'll be glad you did!

DAY 243

"People always told me that my natural ability and good eyesight were the reasons for my success as a hitter. They never talk about the practice, practice, practice."

Ted Williams

God works in different ways, but it is the same God who does the work in all of us. 1 Corinthians 12:6

Are you putting in the work required to be a better player, coach and friend? A better person? Are you working hard to improve and grow each and every day? You should be. Because God is working in you. He doesn't take days or weeks off. He doesn't take breaks. God is always working. And because God is always working, you should be too. Don't take days off. Rely on God, but do the necessary work to ensure that you fulfill the purpose He has placed on your life. Your relationship with God is a partnership. So work together with Him. Every single day.

DAY 244

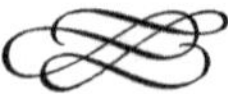

"The trouble with baseball is that it is not played year round."
Gaylord Perry

For everything there is a season, a time for every activity under the sun.

Ecclesiastes 3:1

Spring, Summer, Fall and Winter. The four seasons. And then there's the best season of them all - baseball season! But no matter the season, God created them all. Each season serves a purpose. And so do the times of your life. Those times of joy and happiness, as well as the times of sadness and mourning - God uses them all. For His purpose and for His glory. Just as the seasons change, so does life. Nothing remains the same. Except God's steadfast love for His children. So no matter the season you are currently in, remember that God is always with you!

DAY 245

"Never let your head hang down. Never give up and sit down and grieve. Find another way." Satchel Paige

The Lord is close to the broken-hearted; he rescues those whose spirits are broken. Psalms 34:18

Sometimes life is difficult. Stress, loss and loneliness can leave you on the verge of tears, feeling as though you're going to give up. But instead of hanging your head down, lift it up. And turn to God. He sees you. He hears you. And He cares. God will deliver you from your troubles. He will heal your troubled heart. All you have to do is ask. He is closer than you think.

DAY 246

"Raise the urinals." Daryl Chaney (when asked how management could keep the Braves on their toes)

He makes me as sure footed as a deer, enabling me to stand on mountain heights. Psalms 18:33

Today the enemy is lurking. He is looking to create obstacles and set traps that cause you to stumble and fall. So be on your toes and be aware. And turn to God. For it is He that places your feet on stable ground. He makes you "as sure footed as a deer" and puts you on mountain tops far from evil's grasp. Ask God to strengthen your feet so that you will remain firm in your stand for Him. Today and every day!

DAY 247

"If a man can beat you, walk him." Leroy Paige

And now I make one more appeal, my dear brothers and sisters. Watch out for people who cause divisions and upset people's faith by teaching things contrary to what you have been taught. Stay away from them. Romans 16:17

The intentional walk. A strategic move to set up a favorable defensive situation. It's also a smart move used to avoid the hitter who can beat you. Today's verse advocates for the personal intentional walk. As in walk away. Quickly and intentionally. From those who are not teaching the Truth, because their teachings can lead you astray and cause division. God's Word is unifying. It brings everyone together. In His Kingdom, we are all brothers and sisters. Any preaching or teaching contrary to this should always be avoided. Amen.

DAY 248

"Trying to hit him (Phil Niekro) was like trying to eat jell-o with chopsticks."

Bobby Murcer

I have told you all this so that you may have peace in me. Here on earth you will have many trials and sorrows. But take heart, because I have overcome the world. John 16:33

Life is full of difficult challenges, trials and sorrows. None of us are immune. And all of us will face them. But in the midst of our challenges, this verse brings peace and comfort. Are you experiencing hardship today? If so, find peace as you look to Him. Trust God's Word and gain His peace. Believe His promises and discover His peace. No matter what you may be facing or have faced, Jesus has already overcome it all. He was victorious. And so are you!

DAY 249

"What has benefited me the most is learning I can't control what happens outside of my pitching." Greg Maddux

My thoughts are nothing like you thoughts, says the Lord. And my ways are far beyond anything you could imagine. Isaiah 55:8

We like to be in control. And too often, we think we know best. Even when it comes to what God is doing. Or not doing. When things don't go our way, we second guess God. In our minds, we create an unrealistic God. One that is created in our image, instead of the other way around. God's ways are beyond anything we can ever imagine. And He is in control. Always. So control what you can control and leave the rest to God!

DAY 250

"Whether I'm hitting .100 or .300 I have resolved to at least enjoy every game."

Dale Murphy

Not that I was ever in need, for I have learned how to be content with whatever I have. Philippians 4:11

If you had nothing, would you still be happy? Would you still be at peace? Or do you find that the more you have, the happier you are? Paul's words today come from experience. Imprisoned, shipwrecked and beaten, Paul had experienced loss firsthand. And although he made tents to support his ministry, Paul also relied on financial support from others. Which means sometimes he had plenty. And other times he had little. But in it all, Paul finds that his joy and his peace come from God, not from his material blessings. So whether you have much or little, God is still in control. So be content. Be at peace. And look to Him for all your needs.

DAY 251

"You may glory a team in triumph, but you fall in love with a team in defeat."

Roger Kahn

We love him, because he first loved us. 1 John 4:19

Who, or what, are you in love with? Money? Self? Your favorite team? Or is it Jesus? As with any relationship, falling in love doesn't just happen. It requires intentionality. It requires time and effort. And sacrifice - sacrificing of time and of self. Making that person a priority. And it's no different with your relationship with Jesus. He made you a priority when he willingly sacrificed himself on the cross. Are you making your relationship with Him a priority? Spend time with Him through prayer, study and meditation. And when you do, He will become the one love that will never break your heart!

<h1 style="text-align:center">DAY 252</h1>

"In this game of baseball, you live by the sword and die by it. You hit and get hit. Remember that." Alvin Dark

"Put away your sword," Jesus told him. "Those who use the sword will die by the sword." Matthew 26:52

After Jesus was betrayed by Judas and arrested, Peter drew his sword and cut off the ear of the high priest. This action led Jesus to admonish Peter and speak today's verse to him. Jesus instructed Peter to put down his sword, knowing that his actions could have him arrested and possibly killed. Ironically, those whose lives are full of violence and aggression will usually see their lives end by violent and aggressive means. Simply put, what goes around comes around. Because when you treat others unfairly, you will eventually be treated unfairly. When you talk badly about others, others will talk badly about you. So instead of causing harm to your neighbor, put down your sword and always act in peace and love.

DAY 253

"I don't rate them. I just hit them." Willie Mays

God sent his Son into the world not to judge the world, but to save the world through him. John 3:17

Jesus wasn't sent into the world to judge us. And if that wasn't His job, mission or priority, why should we make it ours? Judgements of others are often rooted in self righteousness. Thinking that you are better than the people you're judging. Comments like "if that were me" or "I would never" come from a condemning spirit. It's not your job. Your job today is to show love and compassion. Just like Jesus did.

DAY 254

"To a pitcher, a base hit is the perfect example of negative feedback." Steve Hovley

If you reject discipline, you only harm yourself; but if you listen to correction, you grow in understanding. Proverbs 15:32

Results are a form of feedback. Negative or positive, they are often an indicator of our previous thoughts, actions and behaviors. Some lead to success. Others to failure and discipline. How do you respond to the different types of feedback you receive? Do you learn from it and make corrections? Or do you reject it, dig your heels in and continue with the same approach? Today's verse teaches us that when we do this we only harm ourselves, and subsequently, the people around us. So when you receive feedback today, humble yourself. Turn to God. And make the necessary changes and adjustments. And then, thank God for the feedback!

DAY 255

"The difference between the impossible and the possible lies in a man's determination." Tommy Lasorda

You grew weary in your search, but you never gave up. Desire gave you renewed strength, and you did not grow weary. Isaiah 57:11

Everyone gets knocked down in life. Usually more than once. And some, more often than others. But the key to getting back up depends on your response. Do you lay there and wallow in self pity, thinking of what could have been and how unfair it seems? Or do you get up and keep going, vowing to overcome the obstacles that you are facing? That is the very definition of determination! It's not easy. And we don't do it alone. Determination comes from within. It comes from God and the power of the Holy Spirit. He forms it in you through your experiences and your trials. So the next time life knocks you down and your circumstances feel impossible to overcome, call on Him. Allow God to pick you up and help you keep going!

DAY 256

"I don't want to play golf. When I hit a ball, I want someone else to go chase it." Rogers Hornsby

Seek the Lord while you can find him. Call on him now while he is near.

Isaiah 55:6

Has it been awhile since you chased after God? Or maybe a better question is, have you ever chased Him? Sure we chase after dreams, goals, our kids and sometimes money. But oftentimes those pursuits leave us exhausted and feeling like we can't chase anything else in life. But God is worthy of your pursuit. He is worth being chased. In fact, a relationship with God is the first thing you should chase each day. Spend time with Him. Talk to Him. Listen to Him. Study the Word. The reward of this pursuit will be better than you could ever imagine!

DAY 257

"Life will always throw you curves, just keep fouling them off. The right pitch will come, but when it does, be prepared to run the bases." Rick Maksian

We can make our plans, but the Lord determines our steps. Proverbs 16:9

Planning out our future is not only wise but it's important too. It allows you to prepare for where you want to go or do or be. But sometimes plans change. Things happen. Mistakes are made. And our perfect plan is perfect no more. But regardless of how or why your plans changed, God is still in control. He is still ordaining your steps. Maybe your original plan was a good one. But God has a better one. Maybe your plan was too limited and God wants to use you in a bigger way. So no matter how your plan changes, keep following Him. Keep fouling off the pitch until you get the one God likes. And when you do, swing for the fences. And be ready to run the bases!

DAY 258

"With the money I'm making, I should be playing two positions." Pete Rose

When someone has been given much, much will be required in return and when someone has been entrusted with much, even more will be required. Luke 12:48

Everyone has been given much. This includes you. Talents, knowledge, wisdom, time and wealth. God has blessed you with one, two or maybe even all of these. How are you using them to glorify God? How are others benefiting from your gifts? Your gifts are not intended to be kept for your own personal enjoyment. They are tools. Tools to be used to further the Kingdom of God. The more spiritual tools you are blessed with, then more will be expected from you. Are you using them in a way that glorifies God? He invested in you; is He getting the appropriate return on His investment?

DAY 259

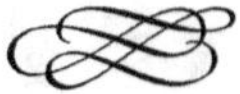

"You always get a special kick on Opening Day, no matter how many you go through. You look forward to it...you think something special is going to happen."

Joe DiMaggio

Faith shows the reality of what we hope for; it is the evidence of things we cannot see. Hebrews 11:1

Anticipation. Expectation. Looking forward to what is coming and believing that it will indeed happen. Do you anticipate Jesus' return in the same way you anticipate the next game? Are you as excited about what God has done for you as you are about your team's big win? You should be. It comes down to living out your faith. And your faith is rooted in who Jesus is, what He's done and what He will do. And it's exciting! So pray with anticipation. Study God's Word with anticipation. And live your life with anticipation. God's promises are true. Wait for it. It's about to happen!

DAY 260

"You have to go broke three times to learn how to make a living." Casey Stengel

The Lord makes some poor and others rich; he brings some down and lifts others up. 1 Samuel 2:7

Regardless of your current financial situation, God is still sovereign and holy. He is still in control. And the status of your bank account has nothing to do with how much God loves you. The One who lifts some up and humbles others is the same God who can change your current situation. He can reverse life situations. He can heal disease, repair relationships and bless you beyond your wildest imagination. Trust Him. Worship Him. And praise Him always, whether you're rich or just getting by!

DAY 261

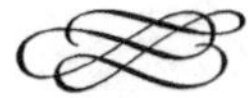

"When I look in the mirror, I look at the enemy. There is no one to blame for this but myself. I should have bought myself a mirror a long time ago." Daryl Strawberry **But let each one examine his own work, and then he will have rejoicing in himself alone, and not in one another. Galatians 6:4**

Sometimes it's not easy to look in the mirror and love the person you see. Especially if you're filled with shame, regret or guilt. These feelings can lead a person to believing that they are unlovable. By others. And by God. But nothing could be further from the truth. God loves you unconditionally. He is constantly working in you and on you. Using your experiences and feelings to mold you into the person He has called you to be. So look in the mirror. Acknowledge your shortcomings. Ask God to help you overcome them. Ask Him to help you love the person you see. And be proud to call yourself a Child of God!

DAY 262

"Everybody knows something and nobody knows everything." Dusty Baker

Fear of the Lord is the foundation of true knowledge, but fools despise wisdom and discipline. Proverbs 1:7

Do you have a teachable spirit? One that is ready, willing and anxious to learn? From others, from your experiences and from God? If so, then you possess a foundation for gaining knowledge and a humble heart. No one has all the answers. Only God does. And when you approach Him with reverence and fear, wisdom will follow. Not fearing God as in being scared, but instead possessing a healthy sense of respect and trust. Trusting that His ways are best. Trusting that His discipline and "no's" will lead you to greater knowledge, understanding and a clearer vision of who He is calling you to be. True knowledge and wisdom come from God. Fear Him. Trust Him. And allow Him to begin teaching you today!

DAY 263

"Losing feels worse than winning feels good." Vin Scully

And we know that God causes everything to work together for the good of those who love God and are called according to His purpose for them.

Romans 8:28

Almost every game in every sport played has a winner and a loser. It's the beauty of the games. And if you've played enough of them, then you have been on both sides - the winning and the losing. Winning feels good. And losing hurts. But it's important to understand that God can often-times teach us more in the valleys than on the mountaintops. We learn about our shortcomings. We learn about the areas of our lives that need improvement. Both on and off the field. And we learn that God is still on the throne as we strive to be more Christlike in every victory and defeat. Cherish the wins. And grow from the losses. Because God is teaching you something!

DAY 264

"Good is not good when better is expected." Vin Scully

So the Lord must wait for you to come to him so he can show you his love and compassion. For the Lord is a faithful God. Blessed are those who wait for his help. Isaiah 30:18

As you begin your day, what are your expectations for this day? To just survive it and get through it? Are you waiting for the next bad thing to happen? Or are you expecting to experience the best of what God has in store for you? Expectations can be dangerous. Because what you are expecting from this day is a reflection of who you are expecting it from. When you expect negative results, then your expectations are from the evil one. But if you expect to experience goodness and blessings, then your expectation is from God. And that's exactly where it should be! God is a good God and He wants to bless you. Every day. But you must expect it. And wait for it patiently. Don't become discouraged and hopeless. Instead, place your hopes and your expectations in Him. Good is never good enough when God can give you better!

DAY 265

"Because we call ourselves Christians, our actions need to reflect Christ."

Clayton Kershaw

But now you need to be holy in everything you do, just as God who chose you is holy. For the Scriptures say, "You must be holy because I am holy."

1 Peter 1:15-16

It's easy to call yourself a Christian. Put a fish bumper sticker on your car, get a cross necklace, buy a Bible and now you're called a Christian. But are you actually living as a Christian should? Do your words, thoughts and actions reflect the love and teachings of Jesus? We are called to live holy lives. Not just on Sundays but all the time. Your life should mirror the holiness of God, living as a shining light in a dark world. As a follower of Christ, you are set apart from the world. Called to live a holy life by the One who chose you first.

DAY 266

"To be the best, you must face the best. And to overcome your fear, you must deal with the best." Barry Bonds

But you are to be perfect, as your Father in heaven is perfect. Matthew 5:48

To be the best, you've got to beat the best. And to be perfect, you must be like the One who is perfect. God knows that it is impossible to be perfect. Our sinful nature makes it impossible for us to achieve perfection. But we can try and strive to be like the only perfect one - Jesus. When the teachings of Christ guide you and lead you, the Holy Spirit will work in you and mature you. In doing so, you will become more Christlike and your relationship with God is strengthened. Strive to be more like Christ today. And if you fall short, talk to God. And ask Him to help you do better tomorrow!

DAY 267

"Those boos really motivate me to make something happen."
Barry Bonds

From there Elisha went up to Bethel. As he was walking along the road, some boys came out of the town and jeered at him. "Get out of here, baldy!" they said. "Get out of here, baldy!" He turned around, looked at them and called down a curse on them in the name of the Lord. Then two bears came out of the woods and mauled forty two of the boys. And he went on to Mount Carmel and from there returned to Samaria. 2 Kings 2:23-25

Everyone has been booed before. Or at the very least had someone cheer their failure. It can be alarming. But how do you respond when the jeers are loud enough for you to hear? Do you quit? Do you become so rattled that you can't perform your duties? Or do you block it out and continue fighting through it? Elisha heard it. But instead of turning around or giving up, he called out to the source of our strength. So the next time the jeers or boos get to you, cry out to God. Whether it's for a curse, for strength or for both, that's your decision. But whatever you do, call on God. He's waiting.

DAY 268

"I never want to sit out. I want to play baseball games."
Matt Kemp

Then Jesus said, "Come to me, all of you who are weary and carry heavy burdens, and I will give you rest." Matthew 11:28

Life is busy. Schedules fill up fast. And the daily grind wears us down, mentally, physically and spiritually. Exhaustion is most definitely real. To the point that sometimes you just want to sit the day out. Or the game. But Jesus gives clear and simple instructions when you begin to feel like this. Go to Him. Because no matter how busy or tired you may be, you can always find rest in Jesus. Rest in Jesus is filled with peace and love. It provides encouragement and comfort, guidance and support. So when life is wearing you down, focus on Jesus. And His rest will be yours!

DAY 269

"You never know who's watching." Don Mattingly

He will not let you stumble; the one who watches over you will not slumber.

Psalms 121:3

It's true. You never know who's watching. Might be a child, a boss, coworkers or even a scout. Or it could be that no one is watching or paying attention to what you're doing. But there is one who is watching over you all the time. And that's your Heavenly Father. Even when you're sleeping, God is watching. When you're working or on the field or spending time with your family and friends, God is watching. Because He loves you. God loves His children. And just like a proud parent who watches over their child, God proudly watches over you! Even when no one else is. Praise be to God!

DAY 270

"If the shortstop makes an error, I am responsible. I let the batter hit the ball."

Pedro Martinez

For we are each responsible for our own conduct. Galatians 6:5

Oftentimes in life, people shun responsibility. Instead they play the blame game instead of taking responsibility for their words and actions. Are you one of those people? In our scripture today, Paul speaks about being responsible for our own actions. Our words. Our conduct. No one else makes you say or do something. It's a personal choice to respond. And if your conduct hurts someone, take responsibility. Acknowledge the hurt. Apologize. Ask God for forgiveness and for the strength to be better next time. We all make mistakes. And when you do, own it. And take responsibility for your conduct.

DAY 271

"I'd rather be a good person off the field than a good baseball player on the field." Bryce Harper

You can identify them by their fruit, that is, by the way they act. Can you pick grapes from thorn bushes, or figs from a thistle? Matthew 7:16

What do you want to be known for today? Your accomplishments and accolades? The money in your bank account? Your level of education? Or would you rather be known for being a good person? The way you treat others, the way you act when facing adversity, possessing a servant's heart that's what makes a good person. Jesus's words warn us about the sheep in a wolf's clothing. Those people who act one way but actually have deceitful intentions. Are you one of those people? If so, today's a great day to change! We're all going to be known for something. So starting today, be known for being a good person! Just like Jesus taught!

DAY 272

"I don't believe in curses. I think you make your own destiny." Manny Ramirez

I knew you before I formed you in your mother's womb. Before you were born I set you apart and appointed you as my prophet to the nations. Jeremiah 1:5

Each day you have the ability to make your own moral choices and decisions. Each day you are responsible for those decisions. And because of this free will, you have the ability to determine your own destiny. Are you choosing to follow Jesus's teachings and examples and live in harmony with God? Or are you making and living by your own rules? God set you apart. To be holy. To be a vessel. To be His. And your destiny depends on your decisions. Choose wisely. Choose to follow Him today and every day!

DAY 273

"Baseball is a simple game. If you have good players and if you keep them in the right frame of mind, then the manager is a success." Sparky Anderson

Keep the decrees, commands, regulations and laws written in the Law of Moses so that you will be successful in all you do and wherever you go.

1 Kings 2:3

Determining success in baseball is easy to see. Highest batting average, most home runs, lowest ERA, wins and losses- they are all determined numerically. But what determines success in our daily lives? The answer may be easier than you think. Obedience to God, advancing His Kingdom and being motivated by love. It's actually quite simple. Being successful in God's eyes has nothing to do with numbers or wins and losses. Instead, it has everything to do with obedience and motivation. Living by His Word. Loving Him and loving others. Give it a try today. Success may be more attainable than you realize!

DAY 274

"You could be a kid for as long as you want when you play baseball." Cal Ripken Jr.

Then he said, "I tell you the truth, unless you turn from your sins and become like little children, you will never get into the Kingdom of Heaven."

Matthew 18:3

Being childlike is different from being childish. Childish behavior reflects immaturity. Childlike behavior reflects humility and trust. And that is exactly what God asks of us - humility and trust. Humbling ourselves and accepting corrections. Trusting Him and His Ways. That's it! Jesus's words are powerful. To His disciples, they were confusing and alarming. But it was a simple example of how you are called to approach God. Humble and trusting, knowing that His ways are best. God's ways are motivated by His love for you! Be motivated today by His love!

DAY 275

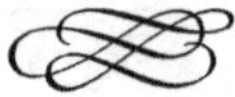

"You don't have to get hits to impress the manager." Bobby Cox

When you pray, don't be like the hypocrites who love to pray publicly on street corners, and in the synagogues where everyone can see them. I tell you the truth, that is all the reward they will ever get. Matthew 6:5

Who will you try to impress today? Who will you show off for? Your boss, your neighbor and your coworkers? When you try to impress others with your words, your actions or your "stuff," it usually backfires. Because their opinions of us usually don't matter, the time spent trying to impress is usually wasted. Jesus warned about praying in such a way that bystanders would be impressed. Loudly and publicly. When your focus is on impressing other people, your focus is not on God and your relationship with Him. God already loves you. You are His child and He is proud of you. He's always impressed with you. And that's all that really matters!

DAY 276

"I've never heard a crowd boo a homer, but I've heard plenty of boos after a strikeout." Babe Ruth

Better to be criticized by a wise person than to be praised by a fool. Ecclesiastes 7:5

Criticism often comes in many forms, both constructive and destructive. And it often comes from different sources. Have you faced criticism recently? How was it presented to you? And most importantly, who did it come from? Learning how to deal with criticism is an essential part of spiritual maturity, because we all face it in our lives. Don't allow the words and opinions of others to change how you feel about yourself. Especially if it comes from someone who is trying to bring you down. Instead, ask God to continue to use you and grow you in a way that glorifies His Kingdom. Make changes if necessary. And focus on the only opinion that really matters - God's!

DAY 277

"Baseball is the greatest game in the world and deserves the best you can give it." Babe Ruth

Whatever you do, do well. For when you go to the grave, there will be no work or planning or knowledge or wisdom. Ecclesiastes 9:10

How much effort are you putting into today? At your job, with your kids, in your relationships? Just enough to get by? Or are you giving everything you have? There are no dress rehearsals with life. This is the only one we get. And those around you, the ones who depend on you, deserve the very best you can give. Regardless of the task you are given, it should be given your full care and attention. As if God gave it to you Himself. If you feel that your efforts are lacking, start with your relationship with Him. Focus on spending more time with Him, reading His Word and experiencing His love. Give God the best of what you have to offer. And once you do this, notice how much more effort you put into the rest of your day. It all starts with Him!

DAY 278

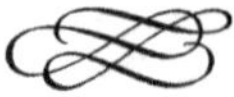

"Don't look back. Something might be gaining on you." Satchel Paige

But Jesus told him, "Anyone who puts a hand to the plow and then looks back is not fit for the Kingdom of God." Luke 9:62

Sometimes it's hard not to look back in life. On our accomplishments, our regrets and the good times and the bad. But when you look back, you often stop moving forward. And growth and development stops. Your calling in life is to follow God. And when you answer the call, there is no turning back or looking back. If you stumble or if you fall, allow God to pick you up. Learn from your past mistakes. But don't look back and dwell on them. The Kingdom of God lies ahead. Set your sights on Him and don't turn back!

<h1 style="text-align:center">DAY 279</h1>

"Show me a guy who's afraid to look bad and I'll show you a guy who can be beat every time." Lou Brock

The Lord is for me, so I will have no fear. What can mere people do to me?

Psalms 118:6

Fear can be paralyzing. Fear of failure. Fear of rejection. Fear of what others might think. Fears of "what if." Fear can stop us in our tracks. And it prevents us from following our heart and our dreams. Overcoming fear isn't easy. But it starts and ends with placing our faith and trust in our Lord and Savior Jesus Christ. Once you realize that God is for you and with you and guiding your steps, fear disappears. He is your protector. He is your Savior. He is The Way. And when you trust Him with every aspect of your life, you will understand that fear is only a tool of the devil, trying to prevent you from becoming the person God is calling you to be. So today, and every day, put your faith in God. Trust Him. And let your fears become a thing of the past!

DAY 280

"Well, baseball was my whole life. Nothing's ever been as fun as baseball."

Mickey Mantle

And when Christ, who is your life, is revealed to the whole world, you will share in all his glory. Colossians 3:4

When you make something your "whole life," it shows. It's evident for all to see. The passion, the commitment, the resolve. It's different than if it's just part of your life. What have you chosen to be your whole life? Baseball? A career? If it's anything other than your relationship with Jesus, it's time to make a change. Other things can be important to you, but nothing should take priority over living a Godly life. Jesus gave His life for you so that you may experience eternal life. He gave His whole life for you. Beginning today, make the decision to give your whole life to Him. And everything else will fall into its rightful place!

DAY 281

"A man has to have goals - for a day, for a lifetime - and that was mine, to have people say "There goes Ted Williams, the greatest hitter who ever lived.""

Ted Williams

Good planning and hard work lead to prosperity, but hasty shortcuts lead to poverty. Proverbs 21:5

Are you living your life with purpose, with plans and determination? With definitive goals? Or are you taking it day by day, making it up as you go? Life is a gift from God. Your talents are as well. And while God is the One who is ultimately in control, your actions can and will determine the outcome, as well your successes and failures. When you choose to live according to God's will for your life, your goals become clear. They prioritize themselves and you will quickly understand what's important in life. Living for Him becomes your goal. And when it does, you learn to respond to life differently. Instead of living a reactionary life, live each day with determination and purpose. Just as God intended.

DAY 282

"I usually take a two hour nap from 1:00 - 4:00." Yogi Berra

And God blessed the seventh day and declared it holy, because it was the day when he rested from all his work of creation. Genesis 2:3

We are a part of a fast paced world. Deadlines, long hours, countless responsibilities. Combined, they leave us tired and exhausted. When was the last time you rested? Or do you live by the saying "I'll sleep when I'm dead?" Jesus rested. So did God. So why shouldn't you? Life can be stressful and overwhelming. And when it is, we find ourselves tired and lacking peace. But in the storms and stresses of life, God is our shelter. He provides us peace. So take time out of your day today and rest in Him. Recharge your batteries. Experience God's peace. And then make it a part of your daily routine!

DAY 283

"A nickel ain't worth a dime anymore." Yogi Berra

For the love of money is the root of all kinds of evil. And some people, craving money, have wandered from the true faith and pierced themselves with many sorrows. 1 Timothy 6:10

There's nothing wrong with having money. And there's nothing unbiblical about wanting to have money. The issue arises when the love of money becomes more important than loving God. And when the desire to acquire money is stronger than the desire to know God. Nothing should ever be more important to you than your relationship with The Father. And whether you are rich by worldly standards or you live a life of poverty, remember to whom you belong. You are a child of God. So today, work hard. Earn an honest living. Enjoy the fruits of your labor. But trust in God's provision. And give Him thanks for what he has blessed you with!

DAY 284

"We weren't trying to walk him; he just wouldn't swing at any bad pitches." Bobby Cox

For he will rescue you from every trap and protect you from deadly disease.

Psalms 91:3

Satan sets out traps each day hoping you will take the bait. Doubt traps, anxiety traps and independence traps, just to name a few. And with each trap, the hope is that you will be overcome with fear and worry to the point that you become paralyzed by that fear. That you will be overcome with negative thoughts and emotions. That your loving heart will become cold and hardened. The traps are everywhere! Don't take the bait! Instead, place your trust in God. Focus on his goodness and mercy. Focus on your loving Father and finding peace and comfort when you call on Him. The enemy's traps are no match for God's love. He knows he doesn't have a chance. But he will continue to set up traps each day, hoping to capture you in a moment of weakness.

But stand strong. Remain steadfast. Focus on God's love. And if you take the bait and become ensnared, call on The Lord to rescue you from the trap!

DAY 285

"It ain't over till it's over." Yogi Berra

When Jesus had tasted it, he said, "It is finished!" Then he bowed his head and gave up his spirit. John 19:30

Comebacks are part of sports, especially in baseball. So until the 27th out is recorded, the game is never over. It's why today's quote from Yogi has always been true - "it's not over till it's over." On the cross, Jesus declared that it was over when he cried out, "it is finished." The unforgiveness you're dealing with - it's finished. The shame and guilt you're experiencing - it's finished too. And the pain and suffering you're feeling - it's finished as well. In other words, it's all over! When they nailed Jesus to the cross, your sins were nailed there too. Jesus's words and His work live on, but your shortcomings died on the cross. Forgiveness is yours. Eternal life is yours. Because of the love Jesus showed that day, His work was completed. But his peace and love will be yours forever!

DAY 286

"They broke it to me gently. The manager came up to me before the game and told me they didn't allow visitors in the clubhouse." Bob Uecker

Let your gentleness be evident to all. The Lord is near. Philippians 4:5

Being gentle doesn't mean that you are soft. Or weak. In fact, it's actually a sign of a Godly man or woman. Gentleness is an important theme in the Bible. Jesus exhibited gentleness in his interactions with others. And you should too. Because it's rooted in a love for our brothers and sisters in Christ. It shows compassion and humility. And it shows that we care. It's not always easy. People can be difficult. Days can be a struggle. And being gentle may be the last quality you want to show when facing these challenges. But Jesus is our example and we are called to follow his ways. So be gentle with your words and actions today. You'll be happy you did!

DAY 287

"Just as nature fills a vacuum, Reggie fills a spotlight." Bob Marshall (on Reggie Jackson)

Don't demand an audience with the king or push for a place among the great. Proverbs 25:6

Some people love being the center of attention. They crave the spotlight and will do anything to get there. The "likes" and the compliments - they feed their ego. It makes them feel important. Are you one of those people? Do you seek out the spotlight and the approval of others? The Bible repeatedly teaches us about the importance of humility. Jesus put others first. And you should too. He reached out to the lowly, the poor and the forgotten. And you should too. Seeking out validation from others is a slippery slope. It means you care more about the opinions of others and will often do anything for their approval. Instead, you should be focused on living for God, following the teachings of Jesus and putting others first. That's all the validation you need!

DAY 288

"Nice guys finish last." Leo Durocher

Never let loyalty and kindness leave you! Tie them around your neck as a reminder. Write them deep within your heart. Proverbs 3:3

Nice guys are what this world needs more of. The cost of being rude is high. It hurts others and it can cost you relationships, jobs and even money. But it costs nothing to be kind. And the payoffs and benefits are amazing. Jesus lived a life of kindness. And we are called to follow his example. In doing so, you will find favor with God and earn the respect of others. So in a world where you can be anything, choose to be kind. It's a choice you'll never regret!

DAY 289

"So many ideas come to you (when slumping) and you want to try them all but you can't. You're like a mosquito in a nudist camp. You don't know where to start."

Reggie Jackson

For I am about to do something new. See, I have already begun! Do you not see it? I will make a pathway through the wilderness. I will create rivers in the dry wasteland. Isaiah 43:19

Today is a new day. A new beginning. And God is about to do something amazing with you. And for you. Your past is just that - your past. Let go of it. Be receptive to what He is doing in your life. Because God, who is faithful, is your future. Trust that He is at work in you and in your life. Seek Him and you will find Him. Ask God to reveal what He's doing. And follow Him. Each and every day.

DAY 290

"I spent three of the best years of my life in the tenth grade." Bob Uecker

Like newborn babies, you must crave pure spiritual milk so that you will grow into a full experience of salvation. Cry out for this nourishment. 1 Peter 2:2

Time is valuable. You never get it back, because once it's gone - it's gone. So where are you spending your time? Video games? Watching TV? Worrying? How much of your time are you spending with God? The key to any strong relationship is directly proportionate to the amount of time spent developing that relationship. And it's no different in your spiritual life. Do you crave time with God? Do you create time in your day for Him? If not, you need to. The only way to strengthen your faith and deepen your understanding of God's Word is to spend quality time with Him each and every day. And today is the best day to start!

DAY 291

"Don't forget to swing hard, in case you hit the ball."
Woodie Held

But watch out! Be careful never to forget what you yourself have seen. Do not let these memories escape from your mind as long as you live! And be sure to pass them on to your children and grandchildren. Deuteronomy 4:9

Forgetfulness. It happens to all of us. We forget to take out the trash. An anniversary. A birthday. An upcoming deadline or test. It's not the end of the world, but it can cause problems. But there are some things that we should never forget. And that is exactly what Moses is telling the Israelites in today's scripture. God is in the miracle business. And we have all seen, experienced or heard of miracles in our lives. We've all experienced the goodness and faithfulness of God. And it shouldn't be forgotten! So the next time you feel unloved or unlucky or feel like God isn't there, remember all that He has done for you. And don't forget how much God loves you!

DAY 292

"You're only young once, but you can be immature forever."
Larry Andersen

When I was a child, I spoke and thought and reasoned as a child. But when I grew up, I put away childish things. 1 Corinthians 13:11

It's not always fun growing up. Priorities change and responsibilities become more demanding. But it's part of life. It's part of the maturation process. And it's a part maturing spiritually as well. It's true that we are taught by Jesus to have "childlike faith," but we must deepen our understanding of scripture as we grow older. As our mind grows, so must our knowledge of The Bible. So must our desire to know Him more. And so must our willingness to serve and love others. As children, we are naturally selfish. But as a maturing Christian, we are called to live a life devoted and dedicated to God. A life where a relationship with The Father is the priority and living out a life of love is our calling. So today, focus on growing up, growing in love and growing your relationship with God!

"It's hard winning a game but it's harder losing one." Chuck Tanner

And we know that God causes everything to work together for the good of those who love God and are called according to his purpose for them.

Romans 8:28

Losing stinks. In life. And in the game of baseball. But it's part of it. Sometimes it's due to poor performance or poor preparation. But sometimes we just get outplayed. The other guy, or the other team, on that particular day, is just better. How do you respond to losing? Hang your head and contemplate quitting? Or do you commit to working harder, grinding out the needed reps to make sure it doesn't happen again? Setbacks in life are similar to losses in sports. They happen. And having the proper mindset is the key to overcoming them. As a child of God, it's important to understand that God uses the good and bad to fulfill His purposes in life. For you. And for His Kingdom. He uses it all, even when it doesn't make sense. Even when it hurts. So keep working. Keep pressing forward. God is using it for your good!

DAY 294

"Close doesn't count in baseball. Close only counts in horseshoes and grenades." Frank Robinson

If you look for me wholeheartedly, you will find me. Jeremiah 29:13

How close do you feel to God today? Does it feel like He's forgotten you or like He's distant? He's not. And He hasn't. He's still there. Still loving you, protecting you and guiding you - just like He promised. God doesn't move away from us. Oftentimes the distance we may feel or experience is because we are the ones who have moved from His presence. God has promised that if we seek Him, we will find Him. He's not hiding from you in your time of need. He's there with you. Waiting for you to call on Him. Waiting for you to turn to Him. God's love and presence is steadfast. Seek Him wholeheartedly, today and every day!

DAY 295

"I was never scared when I had the ball but when I let go I was scared to death." Lefty Gomez

Let me hear of your unfailing love each morning, for I am trusting you. Show me where to walk, for I give myself to you. Psalms 143:8

As humans, our nature is that we like to be in control. Of our lives, our actions and our decisions. Letting go of that control is hard. Really hard. Because it requires faith and it requires trust. It requires putting the outcomes and results in God's hands. When was the last time you were able to do this? Start doing it today. Trust God with this day. And then do it again tomorrow. God loves you more than you know. And He wants you to trust His goodness. He will lead you and guide you and help you fulfill your purpose. Let go of your desire to be in control. And let God show you the way. Do you have enough faith to trust Him?

DAY 296

"He (Jackie Robinson) said baseball was a game you played every day, not once a week." Hank Aaron

As they talked and discussed these things, Jesus himself suddenly came and began walking with them. Luke 24:15

A relationship with God requires commitment and time. Not just once a week or on occasion or when you have a need for Him. But true daily commitment. Spending time in the Word, spending time in prayer and spending time listening to Him. How much time do you spend with God? And how often are you doing it? The strength of your relationship is directly proportional to the time spent in His presence. Strengthen your commitment. Strengthen your relationship. And watch how your life changes for good.

DAY 297

"I'm not afraid of criticism or what somebody may think."
Don Mattingly

But this will be your opportunity to tell them about me. Luke 21:13

Criticism can be harsh. It hurts our pride, creates doubt and can hurt our feelings. Especially if we feel the criticism is unjust. How do you respond to criticism? How do you respond to the person who is criticizing you? People who are critical of others are usually hurting themselves. Trying to protect a vulnerability they possess and project their own insecurities onto you. The natural response is to lash out. Don't. Instead, view the criticism as an opportunity. An opportunity to make changes. But most importantly, view it as an opportunity to show God's love, mercy and grace to the one who is criticizing. As a result, both of you will be better!

"It took me 17 years to get 3000 hits in baseball. It took one afternoon on the golf course." Hank Aaron

The end of a matter is better than its beginning, and patience is better than pride. Ecclesiastes 7:8

We are part of a microwave world. We want things fast. Drive thru. Fast food. Same day delivery. We want it now! But we serve a crockpot God. Crock Pots take time. Usually hours. Start it in the morning, ready for dinner time. It's definitely not fast food. Our walk with God, our spiritual formation is similar. It takes time. And patience. Gaining wisdom and knowledge takes a lifetime of commitment and dedication. Growing your relationship with God doesn't happen overnight. So be patient. Spend time with God every day. Talk to Him. Listen to Him. Spend time in His presence. Today is the best day to start!

DAY 299

"Just take the ball and throw it where you want to. Throw strikes. Home plate don't move." Satchel Paige

So whether we are here in this body or away from this body, our goal is to please him. 2 Corinthians 5:9

Some goals in life are very fluid. They change with the seasons of life. Family goals. Financial and career goals. Goals related to the game of baseball. They all change from time to time. But just as home plate doesn't move, neither should our ultimate goals in life. And that is to live a life that is pleasing to God. This is accomplished when we live in accordance with the calling He has placed on our lives. Bringing glory to His name. Reflecting the Light of Christ. Living out the Gospel each and every day. These should be all of our goals and priorities. And they should never change. What are your goals in life? For today? Do they include living according to God's will and purpose? If so, keep it up! If not, consider adjusting your goals and making God the priority. Everything else will fall into place!

DAY 300

"If you ask me anything I don't know, I'm not going to answer." Yogi Berra

Even fools are thought wise when they keep silent; with their mouths shut, they seem intelligent. Proverbs 17:28

Silence can be uncomfortable. And remaining silent can be difficult. But oftentimes, it's necessary for a variety of reasons. It avoids conflict. It keeps the peace. And it's a part of spiritual maturity. As a maturing believer, learning to listen, think and pray before speaking requires an even tempered demeanor. It requires keeping your emotions in check and under control. Failure to do so often results in unnecessary and avoidable consequences. Challenge yourself today. To think, listen and pray before speaking. And when in doubt, stay quiet. God will give you the words to speak when the time is right!

DAY 301

"I can see how he (Sandy Koufax) won 25 games. What I don't understand is how he lost 5." Yogi Berra

Let those who are wise understand these things. Let those with discernment listen carefully. The paths of the Lord are true and right, and righteous people live by walking in them. But in those paths sinners stumble and fall. Hosea 13:9

Sometimes life is confusing. Sometimes life is hard to understand. And sometimes it's even hard to understand what God is doing. But you are not called to understand God's purposes. You are called to simply trust Him. God will direct your paths. Not through understanding, but through trust. So how do you trust God when you don't understand what He is up to? By remaining anchored in His Word. And reminding ourselves of His promises and constant presence. In doing so, your faith and trust will be affirmed. Then, and only then, can you face the daily storms - even when you don't understand why they are happening.

DAY 302

"Why buy good luggage, you only use it when you travel."
Yogi Berra

And there by the Ahava Canal, I gave orders for all of us to fast and humble ourselves before our God. We prayed that he would give us a safe journey and protect us, our children, and our goods as we traveled. Ezra 8:21

Life is a journey. It can be filled with unexpected challenges and pleasant surprises, detours and shortcuts. Who is guiding you on your journey? The advice of others? Your own selfish desires? Or is God your daily GPS? In order to experience the fullness of life, God must be your pilot. To endure the ups and downs on the journey of life, God must be directing your steps. He must be the one who is in control. Journey through this day with God. Trust His guidance. And learn to view the detours as God's blessings in disguise!

DAY 303

"I have just one superstition. Whenever I hit a home run, I make certain I touch all four bases." Babe Ruth

Do not waste time arguing over godless ideas and old wives' tales. Instead, train yourself to be godly. 1 Timothy 4:7

Are you superstitious? Do you feel that a certain number or an action will bring about bad luck? Or do you feel that certain actions will prevent bad things from happening? If God is in control of your life and the universe, how is this possible? It's not. If God is in control of everything, then it is unreasonable to believe that an outside force or action can change that. Place your faith and trust in God. Not in an old wives' tale or a superstition. So break a mirror. Walk under a ladder. Choose the number 13. Because God is in control!

DAY 304

"Do not deny the impact your life can have on others." Dave Dravecky

For God is not unjust. He will not forget how hard you have worked for him and how you have shown your love to him by caring for other believers, as you still do. Hebrews 6:10

Your words and actions matter. To God and to others. How do you want to be viewed? And remembered? If you are a child of God, if you place your faith and trust in Him, then serving others is an expression of your faith. Speaking words that are edifying. Helping others in need. Loving the unlovable. Someone will be watching you today. Someone will need to see you live out your faith. Someone will need a "God moment." You may not even realize it, but it could potentially change their life. So love and serve God today. Change a life. Impact others. God will see you. And He will not forget!

DAY 305

"No matter what I talk about, I always get back to baseball."
Connie Mack

Do you have the gift of speaking? Then speak as though God himself were speaking through you. 1 Peter 4:11

God speaks in a variety of ways. Through His Word, through prayer, through dreams and through you. Do your words reflect the love, mercy and grace of God? Or do they reflect the cruel, harsh attitudes of the world? Not everyone is blessed with the ability to speak comfortably in public. Not everyone is blessed with a platform to speak. If. you are, use it. Use it to glorify Him. Use it to lift others up. Use it to spread love. So today, whether you are speaking to one person or a large gathering, allow God to speak through you. When you do, you will bring glory to The Father, one word at a time.

DAY 306

"To me, baseball has always been a reflection of life. Like life, it adjusts. It survives everything." Willie Stargell

And the one sitting on the throne said, "Look, I am making everything new!" And then he said to me, "Write this down, for what I tell you is trustworthy and true." Revelation 21:5

Embracing change. It's such a hard concept to grasp. And welcome. But it's necessary. Because change is inevitable. Don't be surprised by it. And don't panic. Instead, keep it in perspective and put your trust in God. He is doing a new thing with you, and in you. Today is a new day. Change is coming. Adjust. And trust. God is with you always, no matter what you're facing!

DAY 307

"The best ballplayer's the one who doesn't think he made good. He keeps trying to convince you." Casey Stengel

Pride ends in humiliation, while humility brings honor. Proverbs 29:23

There's a fine line between confidence and arrogance. Confidence is necessary. Arrogance is dangerous. And it can lead to a humiliating downfall. Where do you land? Confidence? Or arrogance? When God blesses you with a talent, it's important to remain humble. Be confident in your abilities. But remember where your gifts came from - God. He is the giver of all things. He gives. And He takes away. And He blesses you with your talents for a reason - to bring Glory to His name. So use your gifts wisely. Work hard. Get better. Remain humble. And give God the glory!

DAY 308

"A baseball swing is a very finely tuned instrument. It is repetition, and more repetition, then a little more after that." Reggie Jackson

Let me now remind you, dear brothers and sisters, of the Good News I preached to you before. You welcomed it then, and you still stand firm in it.

1 Corinthians 15:1

The Corinthians had heard the Gospel before. They received it. So why was Paul reminding them and continuing to spread the Good News to them again. Because repetition matters. It makes a difference. It helps shape what we believe and what we know. And just like practicing your swing in baseball, repetition is important in our spiritual walk as well. Repetition. Remember. Repeat. It confirms our beliefs. It refreshes our thinking. It's why daily reading is important. It's why daily prayers are imperative. Spend time with God today. And again tomorrow. And the day after tomorrow. Don't stop. Be repetitive. Be committed. And watch your faith grow and your life change. It's a habit worth keeping!

DAY 309

"Baseball is also a game of balance." Stephen King

A false balance is an abomination to the Lord, but a just weight is his delight. Proverbs 11:1

A balanced life is hard to achieve. Kids, practice schedules, work schedules, church commitments. How balanced is your life? Do you feel overwhelmed? On the verge of burnout? If so, it's time to call a timeout. In order to be healthy and productive, it's important that you find a balance in life - one that includes rest and time off. God rested. Jesus rested. So why won't you? Ask God to help you achieve balance in your life. Your body will thank you. And so will your loved ones!

DAY 310

"You can sum up the game of baseball in one word, 'you never know'."

Joaquin Andujar

When you came down long ago, you did awesome deeds beyond our highest expectations. And oh, how the mountains quaked! Isaiah 64:3

Expect the unexpected. In sports. In life. And with God. Because God works in ways we don't look for. He works while we're waiting. And He works in ways we often fear. Too often we place limitations on God. But He is a God of miracles. He is a God who wants us to break free from our limited expectations of His mercy and His goodness. So pray bigger than ever before. Approach Him with a spirit of expectation. Are you praying for a breakthrough? Today might be the day! Because you never know...

DAY 311

"I'm a strong man, and I usually get over hurts and it makes me stronger when I come back." Dusty Baker

The Sovereign Lord is my strength! He makes me as surefooted as a deer, able to tread upon the heights. Habakkuk 3:19

Everyone falls down in life. Some choose to get up. Some don't. The question is why? Is it that they don't want to get up? Are they tired of falling? Afraid of the challenge of getting back up? How do you respond to falling down in life? Comebacks are difficult. But they are necessary. And rewarding. Because they help you become the person that God wants you to be. Life isn't easy. It's filled with ups and downs, peaks and valleys. Life is 10% what happens to you and 90% how you respond. So get up when you fall. Welcome the challenge. Lean on God. And allow Him to lead the way.

DAY 312

"I've told several writers this, and again, I'll get back to it, but if you want to make God smile, tell him your plans." Vin Scully

The Lord says, "I will guide you along the best pathway for your life. I will advise you and watch over you." Psalms 32:8

Sometimes our plans in life aren't the same as God's plans. And it often leads to unnecessary problems and stress, difficulties and disappointments. Life is easier when our plans are aligned with God's plans. So how is this accomplished? Through prayer and study. Learn to listen to God and understand His Word. Seek godly advice. Trust the wisdom and guidance of the counselors God has placed in your life. Acknowledge the Holy Spirit at work within you. Act on the inner conviction you sense in your heart. And lastly, trust God as you move forward. He is leading the way, protecting you from danger. So today, seek out God's plans for your life. Discover it. And follow it. Remember, His way is always best!

DAY 313

"The only thing that is in my control is to win ball games and God is always taking care of me." Dusty Baker

And if God cares so wonderfully for the wildflowers that are here today and thrown into the fire tomorrow, he will certainly care for you. Why have so little faith? Matthew 6:30

God is always taking care of you. No matter the circumstances, no matter the costs - God cares for you. So, why then, do we worry? Because life is stressful. Things happen. Money is tight. Relationships are strained. But worrying is ineffective. It's wasted energy that doesn't fix anything. Instead, rest in knowing that God cares for you more than the birds or the flowers or anything else in His creation. You are His precious child. And if he cares for the wildflowers, imagine how much He cares about you! So instead of worrying, have faith. Trust in knowing that God will provide you with everything you need for this day. Your daily bread. Worrying solves nothing. Trust solves everything!

DAY 314

"A man really determines himself by what he does." Vin Scully

Dear children, let's not merely say that we love each other; let us show the truth by our actions. 1 John 3:18

Your actions speak louder than any words you will ever speak. It's one thing to say that you are following Jesus, but are your actions supporting this claim? No matter where you are or who you are with, your words and actions should always reflect your faith. Jesus taught that we are to love our neighbors. In doing so, we understand that love is not just a noun or a feeling, but it's actually a verb. Love requires action. Following Jesus does too. So today, don't just talk the talk, walk the walk. And let your actions speak for themselves!

DAY315

"I don't know (if they were men or women fans running naked across the field.) They had bags over their heads." Yogi Berra

So we must listen very carefully to the truth we have heard, or we may drift away from it. Hebrews 2:1

Pay attention. We've heard these instructions all our lives. At school, at work, at home. What are you paying attention to? The words and opinions of others? The latest trends on social media? Today's scripture implores us to pay attention to the "truth we have heard." The saving power of Jesus and the grace and mercy of our Father. Life is full of distractions that take our mind away from what's important so it's easy to get sidetracked. Ask God to help you remain focused on what's important- Him. Focus on living out your faith. Living a life full of love and kindness. Being the light in a world of darkness. Don't get distracted today - pay attention to what's important!

DAY 316

"If the world were perfect, it wouldn't be." Yogi Berra

Jesus told him, "If you want to be perfect, go and sell all your possessions and give the money to the poor, and you will have treasure in heaven. Then come, follow me." Matthew 19:21

Perfectionism is a dangerous trait to possess. Because perfection is unattainable and can lead to disaster. In our relationships and in our goals, striving for perfection often drives us to rely on our own strength. And the fear of falling short or disappointing others holds us back from trying new things. In relationships, we hold others to the same standard we hold ourselves to, which also leads to disappointment. Instead of chasing perfection, follow Jesus. Place your hope and expectation in Christ. Find comfort in knowing that God is molding and transforming you into the person He has called you to be. He is bigger than your fears. Do your part, but rely on His strength as He continues to work in your life!

DAY 317

"The only reason I don't like playing in the World Series is I can't watch myself play." Reggie Jackson

You are altogether beautiful, my darling, beautiful in every way.

Song of Songs 4:7

Have you ever watched a video of yourself or seen a picture? Or looked in the mirror? Do you like what you see? You should. Because God likes what He sees when looks at you. And furthermore, He's not concerned with your outer appearance. Rather, He is focused on your heart. Our society is obsessed with outward beauty. But not God. He already thinks you are beautiful. You were created in His image. So today, focus on seeing yourself as God sees you. Stop being critical of you. Because in God's eyes, you really are beautiful!

DAY 318

"There may be people that have more talent than you, but there is no excuse for anyone to work harder than you." Derek Jeter

There are different kinds of spiritual gifts, but the same Spirit is the source of them all. 1 Corinthians 12:4

We all have different gifts and talents. They vary as much as our personalities do. But the source of them all is the same. And the purpose of our gifts and talents is the same as well. To bring glory to God's Kingdom and do good in this world. How are you using your talents? Is it bringing you closer to your sense of purpose? Or are you wasting the gift God has blessed you with? Your talents and gifts are decided upon by God. How you use them is up to you. Don't waste your blessings. And don't miss another opportunity to impact the Kingdom of God!

DAY 319

"Play this game like the 8 year old you used to be, dreaming to play in the show. Heart, passion and fire! Remember where you came from." Bryce Harper

Whom have I in heaven but you? I desire you more than anything on earth.

Psalms 73:25

Our desires can get us in trouble. Or they can help us accomplish our dreams and goals. As you read these words, where are your desires leading you? When your desire is to know God more intimately and to dwell in His presence, you will find everlasting joy. You will find that your life has purpose. There are other things that are important in life. But nothing should be more desirable and important than knowing Jesus and loving him. When you desire a relationship with Him, His desires become yours. And in doing so, your life is filled with love and mercy and joy. What a great life to live!

DAY 320

"Hustle is just playing the game right." Jimmy Rollins

I want to do what is good, but I don't. I don't want to do what is wrong, but I do it anyway. Romans 7:19

Do the right thing. Play the game the right way. Sounds simple, but it's hard to do. Why? Because our flesh and our earthly desires often get in the way. Our wants and attitudes interfere with our ability to do good. Laziness, selfishness and a lack of focus can all keep us from doing the right thing. On the field and in life. When faced with not doing the right things, turn to God. Ask for His direction and guidance. Ask for forgiveness. And approach the opportunity with gratitude, being thankful that God gave you the opportunity to live out your faith. To play another game. And to do things the right way.

DAY 321

"Deep down, it's all baseball, no matter what kind of geometrical shape you play it with." Vernon D. Burns

He told them to take nothing for their journey except a walking stick - no food, no traveler's bag, no money. Mark 6:8

Sometimes we tend to make life more complicated, more cluttered than God intended. Indeed, life has its share of challenges. But many are self created. We fill our minds with stressful thoughts, worrying about the why's, the how's and the when's of life. We stockpile clothes and shoes and boxes in our closets, because what if we need it one day? And in the process, we cloud our vision on the goodness of God. Jesus sent his disciples out with nothing but a walking stick. Their journey would be challenging but he insisted they embark on it simply. Relying on God to provide for their needs and enabling them to recognize His blessings along the way. The same is true for you today. Keep life simple. Don't make it more difficult than it needs to be. Focus on God and not on the "stuff" that clutters your closets and your mind.

DAY 322

"I ain't never had a job, I just always played baseball." Satchel Paige

The Lord God placed the man in the Garden of Eden to tend and watch over it. Genesis 2:15

We all have a purpose to fulfill. Whether it's through a job or a calling, we have a responsibility to fulfill that purpose. What's yours? Some people have the opportunity to play baseball for a living while entertaining us and glorifying God in the process. Others have jobs that are less public, but their purpose is the same - to glorify God. Adam's job was to tend and watch over the Garden of Eden. God gives each one of us different responsibilities. And no matter the tasks, the end goal is the same. To bring glory to the Kingdom of God. Your job is a blessing and an opportunity. Don't waste it.

DAY 323

"Baseball is more than a game. It's like life played out on a field."

Juliana Hatfield

Don't be afraid, for I am with you. Don't be discouraged, for I am your God. I will strengthen you and help you. I will hold you up with my victorious right hand. Isaiah 41:10

Baseball can be a wild and crazy game. Life can be too. It's easy to navigate life when things are going smoothly. When the breaks go in your favor, when the ball bounces your way. When it feels like you're winning, life feels easy. But what about when things don't go your way? When it feels like the wheels are falling off and you can't catch a break? Because that happens too. Sometimes more frequently than we care to experience. What do you do when life plays out in such a way that you feel as though you're losing? Quitting is never an option, so we remember the words of today's scripture. God is with us. He is our God and

He strengthens us and helps us. Always. He doesn't take days off. He doesn't take plays off. In our victories and in our discouraging losses, He is there. Call on Him. Rely on Him. He's is always there to help.

DAY 324

"I love L.A. but you can get into a lot of trouble out here."
Matt Kemp

Watch your tongue and keep your mouth shut, and you will stay out of trouble. Proverbs 21:23

Stay out of trouble. It's something we've heard since we were kids. And it still applies as adults. Unfortunately in today's society, trouble seems to be everywhere. Godless people. Unsafe neighborhoods. Reckless drivers. So much of it is out of our direct control. But there is trouble that we can control and avoid. And that's the trouble caused by our words. When we aren't mindful of the words we speak, we create trouble and drama. Words spoken in anger destroy friendships. Words spoken carelessly stir up gossip and create division. And all of it can be avoided if we learn to watch our mouths. God gave you a voice and a platform. Use them wisely. Use them to proclaim the Gospel. Use them to build others up and comfort them when needed. There's enough trouble in the world as it is. Don't create more with your words!

DAY 325

"I guess my thermometer for my baseball fever is still a goosebump." Vin Scully

Praise him for his mighty works; praise his unequaled greatness! Psalms 150:2

God is good! God is great! And His mighty works often leave us in awe. Miracles, grace, mercy, love, joy and peace - He is the source of them all! God's greatness often leaves us speechless. Because in the midst of difficult times and in the moments of unfiltered success, God is in the middle of it all. So the next time you find yourself questioning God's presence, take a step back. Say a prayer and look around at His creation. What you see and what you feel just might give you goosebumps!

DAY 326

"When you've learned to believe in yourself, there's no telling how good a player you can be. That's because you have a mental edge." Rod Carew

Though a mighty army surrounds me, my heart will not be afraid. Even if I am attacked, I will remain confident. Psalms 27:3

Self confidence is a slippery slope. Self confidence left unchecked leans towards arrogance and a belief that "I" am the reason I am successful. But self confidence, rooted in the belief that God is the source of your strength and your talent, is a good thing. Where does your self confidence lie? Which side do you stand on? Believing in yourself is directly related to your faith in God. Understanding that God is in control and that He blesses you with your gifts is reason to be confident. And grateful. Praise be to God!

DAY 327

"Sweat plus sacrifice equals success." Charlie Finley

And don't forget to do good and to share with those in need. These are the sacrifices that please God. Hebrews 13:16

It takes a lot of sacrifice to be a great baseball player. You have to be willing to give up time with friends and free time, as you fully commit yourself to achieving your goals. Partial commitment leads to partial success and partial accomplishments. To be great, you must be all in. You must be willing to give up something now in order to accomplish your future goals. The same is true with your faith and your relationship with God. God desires an intimate relationship with you. How badly do you want one with Him? Are you willing to make sacrifices in order to spend time with Him each day? Through study. Through prayer. Through meditation. Are you willing to turn from the ways of today's world and stand up for the Kingdom of God? It may cost you. Is it worth it to you? Is the sacrifice worth the end goal of having a deeply intimate and personal relationship with Jesus? The answer is yes! Do good. Make sacrifices. And enjoy the journey as you work to accomplish your goals in life!

DAY 328

"Work like you don't need the money. Love like you've never been hurt. Dance like nobody's watching." Satchel Paige

Love never gives up, never loses faith, is always hopeful, and endures through every circumstance. 1 Corinthians 13:7

Love is the greatest feeling in the world. Being loved and loving someone - there's nothing like it! Whether it's a feeling of romantic love or the feeling of loving a family member or a friend, love is powerful. It is the very essence of God. It involves forgiveness. It involves repentance. And it involves reconciliation. As a believer, you are called to love. Not just the people you like, but your neighbors, enemies and even strangers. God loved you first, so that you may love others. It's not always easy. But it's necessary as a Child of God. God forgives and still loves us through our faults. And you are called to do the same!

DAY 329

"No one goes there nowadays, it's too crowded." Yogi Berra

We no longer see your miraculous signs. All the prophets are gone, and no one can tell us when it will end. Psalms 74:9

Life can be confusing. The words we hear, the actions of others, our circumstances in general. None of it makes sense. It leaves us frustrated and feeling helpless. When you begin to feel this way, pray. Prayer is a powerful tool. And it's your best and only option. Ask God for clarity. Ask Him for the strength to endure. Learn to view your situation as an exercise in faith and as an opportunity to grow and learn. You may not understand your current circumstances right now but one day you will. Until then, choose to trust God.

DAY 330

"It was impossible to get a conversation going, everyone was talking too much."

Yogi Berra

A time to tear and a time to mend. A time to be quiet and a time to speak. Ecclesiastes 3:7

Silence is golden. It protects our thoughts. And often keeps us from hurting other people's feelings. True enough, there are times when we need to speak up. But only after prayerful reflection. Only after asking God to speak through us, to give us the right words and the right opportunity to speak. Conflicts often arise because of careless words and harsh responses. Learn to control your tongue. Train yourself to pray before speaking. And understand that some things are better left unsaid.

DAY 331

"Ain't no man avoid being born average, but there ain't no man got to be common." Satchel Paige

You have been set apart as holy to the Lord your God, and he has chosen you from all the nations of the earth to be his own special treasure.

Deuteronomy 14:2

As followers of Christ, we were created to be "set apart." We are called to be different from the rest of the world. Not just "common," but created for a particular purpose. You were chosen to work for the King. To advance His Kingdom. And God has equipped you for your calling with different gifts and talents. You are not like the rest of the world. You are different. And that is a good thing!

DAY 332

"It's like deja vu all over again." Yogi Berra

History merely repeats itself. It has all been done before. Nothing under the sun is truly new. Ecclesiastes 1:9

Feelings of deja vu can leave you in awe. Whether triggered by a particular sight, smell, taste or sound, the experience can leave you speechless. So can an encounter with God. When you pursue God relentlessly, when you desire to live in His presence, the results will leave you in awe. God wants you to experience the fullness of His love and joy. He wants you to experience the peace that surpasses all understanding. Do you want that for yourself and for your family? If so, pursue Him. Allow yourself to be consumed by a need and a desire to live close to God. The results will leave you speechless!

DAY 333

"I'd like to be able to light the fire a little bit." Reggie Jackson

I have come to set the world on fire, and I wish it were already burning!

Luke 12:49

Are you on fire for Jesus? Is your soul yearning to be in a close relationship with him? To be on fire for Jesus means that you have a strong faith. That you want to know him more. That you want to live for him. A soul on fire for Jesus cannot be extinguished by any external source because the fire burns from within. So today, be on fire for Jesus! Pray to him. Spend time with him. Fan the flame that burns within you and let it spread! Be the spark that ignites the flame in those around you!

DAY 334

"Pair up in threes." Yogi Berra

Then the Lord God said, "It is not good for the man to be alone. I will make a helper that is just right for him." Genesis 2:18

You were created to be in partnership and relationship. With God. And with others. Life can, indeed, be lonely at times. But God did not create you to live a life of loneliness. Sure, sometimes you may want to be alone. Even Jesus felt this way. But there is a difference between loneliness and desiring solitude. God created men and women to be together for companionship, love and friendship. And He gave us neighbors to lend a helping hand. Be mindful of the people God places in your life. They are there for a reason and a purpose. Maybe for a season. Maybe for a lifetime. Only God can reveal that to you. But always remember, God did not create you for loneliness!

DAY 335

"Pitchers, like poets, are born, not made." Cy Young

Jesus replied, "I tell you the truth, unless you are born again, you cannot see the Kingdom of God." John 3:3

The concept of being "born again" can, at first glance, seem confusing and virtually impossible. But it's actually quite simple. Being "born again" refers to a spiritual rebirth, not a physical rebirth. When you are born again, you are given a fresh start at life because of God's amazing love and forgiveness. This new beginning is so complete that it results in a life of hope, faith and love. Jesus gave us new life when he sacrificed his life for our sins. We were made new. Accept the opportunity to be born again and live your life surrounded by God's presence, love, mercy and grace!

DAY 336

"I couldn't quit, because of all the kids, and the blacks and the little people pulling for me. I represent both the underdog and the overdog in our society."

Reggie Jackson

God chose things despised by the world, things counted as nothing at all, and used them to bring to nothing what the world considers important.

1 Corinthians 1:28

Our society loves the story of the underdog. The hardships, the uphill battles, the overcoming. God loves the underdog too! He loves using the underdog to bring glory to His name. Have you ever felt like an underdog? Felt like the odds were against you? Like the uphill climb was too steep to overcome? Then you are just the one God is looking for! Place your faith and trust in Him. Allow Him to use your circumstances and your situation to mold you into the person he has called you to be. Let God raise you out of your environment and use you for good. Not to glorify you, but to glorify Him. Don't give up. Don't accept that it's over or that God is done with you. He uses underdogs like you everyday. Let today be your day!

DAY 337

"In the building I live in on Park Avenue, there are ten people who could buy the Yankees, but none of them could hit the ball out of Yankee Stadium."

Reggie Jackson

I can do nothing on my own. I judge as God tells me. Therefore, my judgment is just, because I carry out the will of the one who sent me, not my own will.

John 5:30

You have special gifts and talents that are only unique to you. You have been blessed with the ability to do things that no one else can do. But always remember the source and the giver of those gifts and talents - God. And also remember that the success of your endeavors is closely tied to God as well. Even Jesus understood this concept. Jesus knew that he could only perform miracles, cast judgment and heal because he sought to do the will of God, not his own will. The success of his mission was directly connected to his intimate relationship with the Father. So why would your success be any different? Ask God to reveal His will for your life to you. Ask Him for opportunities to use your gifts and talents in such a way that glorifies Him. And always remember that you can do nothing on your own!

DAY 338

"If the people don't want to come out to the ballpark, nobody's going to stop 'em." Yogi Berra

Now listen! Today I am giving you a choice between life and death, between prosperity and disaster. Deuteronomy 30:15

Each day is filled with choices. What to wear, what to eat, where to go and what to say. The choice is yours. So is the decision to follow God. No one can force you and no one can stop you. Following God is a choice. Have you made the decision to follow Him? Have you decided who you are serving this day and every day? Each day you have a chance to serve God or serve your own selfish desires. Choose wisely!

DAY 339

"When you unwrap a Reggie Bar, it tells you how good it is."
Catfish Hunter (on Reggie Jackson)

Let someone else praise you, not your own mouth - a stranger, not your own lips. Proverbs 27:2

Do you allow your actions and treatment of others to speak for themselves? Or do you constantly feel the need to offer your own self commentary? Bragging and boasting can be dangerous. And harmful. Without realizing it, self promotion can actually put others down. Instead, remain humble. Avoid self praise. Allow your treatment of others to speak louder than the words you speak about yourself. People will notice. And so will God!

DAY 340

"Play every game as if your life depended on it. It just might."
Casey Stengel

And this same God who takes care of me will supply all your needs from his glorious riches, which have been given to us in Christ Jesus. Philippians 4:19

Life is unpredictable. The weather. Traffic. The actions and words of others. Nothing can be counted on. Everyone and everything is uncertain. This definitely makes for some difficult days. But in this world full of uncertainty, there is One who can be counted on. One who is dependable. God. God will never leave you. He won't forget you. And he'll never turn away from you. In the midst of your crazy times, God is always there. Depend on Him. Rely on Him. Even when you don't understand or agree with your circumstances, depend on God to lead you through. Depend on Him to provide you peace and comfort. Depend on Him as if your life depended on it. It just might…!

DAY 341

"Well, if you can deal with 200 strikeouts, and he can deal with 200 strikeouts, he's going to hit 15 home runs and 15 more fly balls that are going to land on the other side of the fence." Reggie Jackson (speaking to George Steinbrenner about Aaron Judge)

When you go through deep waters, I will be with you. When you go through rivers of difficulty, you will not drown. When you walk through the fire of oppression, you will not be burned up; the flames will not consume you.

Isaiah 43:2

Endurance and perseverance. Words we often hear, but secretly hope we hope we never have to exhibit. Because if we do, in all likelihood, we have faced difficulties and hardships in life that have almost broken us. But in the midst of the storm, in the trials of life, God's promises ring true. He will be with you and the fire will not consume you. And through it all, your faith will be strengthened. You will deal

with difficulties in life. But God will see you through them.
So keep swinging and don't give up!

DAY 342

"Andre Dawson has a bruised knee and is listed as day-to-day." Vin Scully

Lord, remind me how brief my time on earth will be. Remind me that my days are numbered - how fleeting my life is. Psalms 39:4

When dealing with injuries, baseball players are often listed on the injury report as "day-to-day." But then again, aren't we all? Each of us are always listed as day to day because our days are indeed numbered. Our time on earth is brief. And tomorrow is never promised. Knowing that tomorrow isn't promised, how will you approach this day? Will you dwell on hurts and disappointments from the past? Or will you commit yourself to being better today? Will you proceed with bitterness and anger or will you move ahead with love and forgiveness in your heart? Life is short as it is. Living with regrets and sadness only shortens those days. So commit this day to God. Walk with Him. Grow with Him. And enjoy this beautiful day that He has created. It's God's gift to you!

DAY 343

"You can almost taste the pressure now!" Vin Scully

If you fail under pressure, your strength is too small. Proverbs 24:10

Pressure is part of baseball. Crucial at-bats. Late inning heroics. Bases loaded jams. Some players rise to the occasion. Others crumble under the pressure. The same is true in life. Which type of player are you? When faced with pressure, humble yourself. Turn to God. And understand that God uses these moments to strengthen your faith and deepen your relationship with Him. Pressure is part of life. Use it to your advantage!

DAY 344

"It's easier to pick off a fast runner than to pick off a lazy runner." Vin Scully

Then the Lord's anger was aroused against Uzzah, and he struck him dead because he had laid his hand on the Ark. So Uzzah died there in the presence of the Lord. 1 Chronicles 13:10

Enthusiasm and taking initiative are good qualities to possess. But sometimes it crosses the line. And when it does, it can get us in trouble. Just like it did Uzzah in today's scripture. Of all the things you may strive to be, being overzealous should not be one. Learn to be patient. Learn to sense God's presence and when He is nudging you to move forward and when He is telling you to wait. Going before God and trying to lead the way can be dangerous. So always remember that God is in control. Not you. He can and will use you to bring glory to His name. But learn to wait until your number is called!

DAY 345

"The trick is growing up without growing old." Casey Stengel

Meanwhile, the boy Samuel grew taller and grew in favor with the Lord and with the people. 1 Samuel 2:26

Growth is part of life. Physical growth, mental growth and spiritual growth. Often referred to as maturity, it all comes down to growth. Sometimes as we grow, we grow apart from the people we were once close to. Friends, family members and teammates. As our interests and priorities change, so do the relationships that were once important to us. One relationship that should never become distant is your relationship with God. As you grow stronger, your relationship with Him should grow as well. Continue to grow. Continue to mature. Both physically and spiritually. And when you do, you will grow in favor with your Heavenly Father!

DAY 346

"You can't predict baseball Suzyn!" John Sterling

What you ought to say is, "If the Lord wants us to, we will live and do this or that." James 4:15

Many people try to predict the future. Their plans, jobs, games and outcomes. But life is unpredictable. And so is the game of baseball. Instead of wasting time with predictions, focus on the process. Focus on what you can control because oftentimes, the outcome is out of your control. We don't know the future. And try as you may, you cannot predict it. So why waste time trying to figure it out? Instead, invest time in your relationship with God. Invest in the process of getting better. Because ultimately, the outcome is out of your control. Only God knows that. Be prepared, both spiritually and physically, for the next game, the next moment and the next opportunity. And leave the results up to God!

DAY 347

"A curveball is not something you can pick up overnight. It took me years to perfect mine." Bob Gibson

This will continue until we all come to unity in our faith and knowledge of God's Son that we will be mature in the Lord, measuring up to the full and complete standard of Christ. Ephesians 4:13

Indeed, a curveball is not learned overnight. And neither is wisdom and spiritual maturity. It takes time. Lots of it. Are you dedicating time to grow each day in your relationship with God? Through prayer and study and meditation. Are you taking the necessary steps to cultivate a meaningful relationship with Him? Because if you aren't growing each day, you are remaining stagnant and settling for less. Regardless of where you are in life, there's always room to grow and become more like Jesus. So continue to pursue wisdom and healthy study habits. Continue to pursue a deeper relationship with God each and every day, so you can become the person He created you to be. But don't forget, it won't happen overnight!

DAY 348

"Bob Gibson pitches as though he's double parked." Vin Scully

Enthusiasm without knowledge is no good; haste makes mistakes.

Proverbs 19:2

Do you spend the majority of your day hurrying from place to place? Trying to make things happen when you think they should happen? If so, it's time to take a step back and relax. Take a breath. This type of living creates anxiety and worry and often leads to mistakes and exhaustion. God's not in a hurry. And neither was Jesus. Yet His timing is perfect. Never late. And always on time. So today, trust God. Trust His timing. Trust that He will do His work at the right time. Be ready to do your part when called upon. But slow down. And enjoy this precious day He has blessed you with!

DAY 349

"I didn't just show up for work, as has sometimes been said, I also showed up to work." Cal Ripken, Jr.

We must quickly carry out the tasks assigned us by the one who sent us. The night is coming, and then no one can work. John 9:4

Showing up for work is admirable. But showing up to work is even better. And there's a huge difference! Jesus showed up to work. He came into this world knowing His tasks. Just being here wasn't good enough. Jesus had work to complete. And so do you! Your work today is to allow the light of Christ to shine through you onto the paths of others. Lend a helping hand. Listen to the needs of your coworkers. Pray for those who are hurting. Your opportunities may be limited today so make the most of each one you have!

DAY 350

"You win a few, you lose a few. Some get rained out. But you got to dress for all of them." Bob Gibson

So you, too, must keep watch! For you don't know what day your Lord is coming. Matthew 24:42

We hear it all the time on the baseball field - "Be ready!" Be ready for the bunt, the squeeze play, the stolen base, the curveball. Be prepared for whatever the situation calls for. And it's the same way in life. Be ready. Be prepared to help someone out. Be prepared for the storm and the possible loss of power. Be prepared for the worst case scenario. Just be ready. Life is all about being ready and being prepared. Sometimes for the things that we know are coming and sometimes for the uncertainties of life. And although the timing may be uncertain, we all know that one day we will be called home to heaven. So you must be ready. Live each day in a way that pleases God and imitates the life of Jesus, so that one day you will hear Him say, "Well done, good and faithful servant!"

DAY 351

"I have discovered in 20 years of moving around a ballpark, that the knowledge of the game is usually in inverse proportion to the price of the seats." Bill Veeck

Intelligent people are always ready to learn. Their ears are open for knowledge. Proverbs 18:15

Are you a know-it-all? Someone who thinks they know everything and have all the answers? If so, it's a dangerous way to live. Life is a journey of learning. And so is your relationship with God. As a believer, your day is full of opportunities to gain knowledge. About life. And about your Heavenly Father. When you believe that you have all the answers, you miss out on opportunities to gain wisdom. Approach this day with humility. Approach it with a desire and a hunger to know more and learn more. God wants you to seek Him daily. He wants you to seek out the treasures that are found in His Word. Study. Pray. Seek out the wisdom of others. Grow your knowledge of the Lord, starting today!

DAY 352

"A pitcher has to look at the hitter as his mortal enemy."
Early Wynn

Protect me from wicked people who attack me, from murderous enemies who surround me." **Psalms 17:9**

The writer of today's verse, David, found himself surrounded by men who were looking to harm him and ultimately kill him. David would later describe them as deadly and dangerous as a lion. Likely written as he was facing persecution from King Saul, David knew that only God could protect him. Are you surrounded by the enemy today? Are you facing a situation that only God can deliver you from? If so, cry out to God! Go to Him in prayer. Acknowledge your helplessness and need for His intervention and trust Him to lead you through it. Unfortunately, evil does exist in the world today and people will attack you. But God is for you! He will lead you through your trials. He will teach you and he will exalt you. And as He does, He will be glorified!

DAY 353

"There's nothing to it. Baseball isn't that hard." Red Schoendiest

If the world hates you, remember that it hated me first. John 15:18

Contrary to today's quote, baseball is hard. Throwing and catching may be easy, but hitting a 95 MPH fastball is anything but! It requires dedication, perseverance and lots of resolve. So does following Jesus. Because when you commit to following him, you may experience loss. But the gain is so much greater! You may lose friends and family, but you will gain eternal life and peace. The world may hate you and your new ways. But Jesus will always love you. Don't forget, the world hated him first. Following Jesus may seem hard and challenging. You may even consider giving up and returning to your old ways and habits. But don't. Choosing to follow Jesus each day of your life may seem hard, but it will be the best decision you'll ever make!

DAY 354

"The bigger the contract, the bigger the responsibility." Pedro Martinez

The master was full of praise. "Well done, my good and faithful servant. You have been faithful in handling this small amount, so now I will give you many more responsibilities. Let's celebrate together!" Matthew 25:21

You have been blessed with spiritual gifts and talents that are unique to you. No one else can do exactly what you have been called to do. So how are you utilizing your gifts and talents? Are you using them to fulfill God's purpose in your life? Or have you squandered those opportunities? Have you been faithful? To be faithful is to be committed to your calling and purpose. To be faithful is to be dependable and trustworthy. When you are, you will be blessed. You will be rewarded with more opportunities and responsibilities than you can ever imagine. So be faithful. Be a good steward of your God given talents. God has called you into His service. And He wants to celebrate with you. Are you up for the challenge?

DAY 355

"The pitcher has to find out if the hitter is timid. And if the hitter is timid, he has to remind the hitter he's timid." Don Drysdale

Such love has no fear, because perfect love expels all fear. If we are afraid, it is for fear of punishment, and this shows that we have not fully experienced his perfect love. 1 John 4:18

To be timid is to be fearful. And fear comes from hearing the lies of the devil. It's not from God. Because God provides a spirit of love and peace, which leads to optimism and hope. What are you timid about today? What are you fearful of? Have you taken those worries and concerns to God today? The beginning of the end of fear starts with prayer. Be bold with your prayers. Ask for the courage to face your fears, knowing that God is with you always. And He's only a prayer away!

DAY 356

"The only thing that keeps this organization from being recognized as one of the finest in baseball is wins and losses at the major league level." Chuck Lamar

It's not good to eat too much honey, and it's not good to seek honors for yourself. Proverbs 25:27

Recognition. Our pride desires it. It makes us feel good. Makes us feel like others appreciate us and see how great we are. But seeking out recognition is dangerous. It can lead to arrogance and an inflated ego. It doesn't mean that the good deeds aren't good. But drawing attention to your good deeds means you get the glory. Not God. So instead of seeking out the recognition and taking the credit, give the glory to God. Thank Him for the opportunity and the ability to complete it. But never take the credit. It belongs to God!

DAY 357

"If you do a job, do it right or there is no point." Cal Ripken, Jr

Work brings profit, but mere talk leads to poverty. Proverbs 14:23

Mundane tasks. Busy work. So many times our work and jobs seem pointless. But instead of going through the motions just to get it done, make a conscious decision. Make the choice to work in such a way that is pleasing to God. Because regardless of the tasks, you are working for Him, not another man (or woman.) You were not created to do the bare minimum in life. To just slide by or get by. You were created to work hard. You were created to glorify God!

DAY 358

"If you don't think too good, don't think too much." Ted Williams

Guard your heart above all else, for it determines the course of your life.

Proverbs 4:23

Believe it or not, your heart and your mind are connected. If you feel it in your heart, you'll think it in your mind. And if you think it in your mind, you'll feel it in your heart. So guard them both. There is no guarantee that positive thoughts will always lead to positive outcomes. But it's a safe bet that negative thoughts will generally lead to negative results. So be careful to not allow your overthinking and overanalyzing to prevent you from doing good and carrying out God's perfect plan. You have been chosen by God to do His will and reflect His love in all you say and do. And your thoughts today should reflect that!

DAY 359

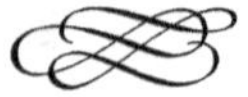

"There are two theories on hitting the knuckleball. Unfortunately neither of them works." Charley Lau

Ask me and I will tell you remarkable secrets you do not know about things to come. Jeremiah 33:3

A knuckleball can be confusing and uncertain. Virtually impossible to hit, even the best hitters in baseball can look foolish in the batter's box. It's almost like life. Unpredictable. Constantly changing. Also making us feel foolish. It can be frustrating because we don't know where our lives are going or what God is doing. But you have been called to trust God and wait for Him expectantly. Waiting for Him to reveal those amazing things that we may not yet know or comprehend. How is this possible? Through prayer. Through earnestly seeking His wisdom and guidance. In doing so, God will reveal Himself and His plans for your life. So the next time life has you feeling like you're swinging and missing a knuckleball, call on God to help you. He's waiting....

DAY 360

"Running a ball club is like raising kids who fall out of trees."
Tom Trebelhorn

A third time he asked him, "Simon, son of John, do you love me?" Peter was hurt that Jesus asked the question a third time. He said, "Lord, you know everything. You know that I love you." Jesus said, "Then feed my sheep."

John 21:17

You have been tasked with the responsibility to lead. As a father, a coach, a teammate or a boss. You have been called to lead. Have you shied away from your responsibilities as a leader? Maybe you feel unworthy or unprepared or even ill-equipped. But God is counting on you! He has given you the tools, the experience and most importantly, the resources to be a leader. God is always present to lead you as you lead others. Are you following His lead? Are you cultivating a relationship with Him that will help you in your role as a leader? If not, today is a great day to start. Follow God. Live out the Scriptures. Treat others with love and kindness and mercy. And don't be surprised when the people around you begin following your example!

DAY 361

"I was the worst hitter ever. I never even broke a bat until last year when I was backing out of the garage." Lefty Gomez

This is a trustworthy saying, and everyone should accept it: "Christ Jesus came into this world to save sinners "—and I am the worst of them all.

1 Timothy 1:15

God's love is transformational! It's not just for the people who are "doing good." It's for everyone. The best of the best and the worst of the worst. No one is too far gone to be touched by the love of God. Jesus was sent to earth to die on the cross for the forgiveness of sins for everyone, not just a select few. No matter how you view yourself, no matter how society views you or labels you, God's love and forgiveness is for you! So claim it! Live in it. Bask in it. Let the love of God warm your heart. Let His Spirit permeate your soul. Allow the light of Christ to shine through you. Today and everyday!

DAY 362

"I know a baseball star who wouldn't report the theft of his wife's credit cards because the thief spends less than she does." Joe Garagiola

The thief's purpose is to steal and kill and destroy. My purpose is to give them a rich and satisfying life. John 10:10

Joy robbers are everywhere. They seek to steal your joy, destroy your enthusiasm and kill your peace of mind. And they come in different forms. Some are strangers who don't know anything about you. And others are friends, family and coworkers who know everything about you. They are fueled by jealousy and unhappiness and look to spread their misery to everyone around them. Unfortunately, oftentimes they are unavoidable. We encounter them on a daily basis. But Jesus is the remedy. Jesus offers comfort and peace. He is there to encourage you. He's there to walk with you in the midst of your difficult times. Don't allow others to steal your joy. Instead, allow Jesus to be your joy!

DAY 363

"The Mets have found ways of losing that I never knew existed." Casey Stengel

Your own ears will hear him. Right behind you a voice will say, "This is the way you should go," whether to the right or left. Isaiah 30:21

Have you ever tried to find your way to a particular destination without the use of directions? Sometimes you arrive successfully. Sometimes you get lost. Other times you end up on paths that you never knew existed. It's the same way with life. When you attempt to find your own way and plot your own course, it usually leads to disappointment. And feelings of being lost. It can be scary and disheartening. But God has promised each of us that if you will lean on Him and listen to His voice, He will direct you. He will show you the way you should go. He has a plan for your life. But in order to get there, you must be obedient. God knows the stumbling blocks and obstacles you will encounter. By listening to Him, you can avoid them. Or at the very least, you will be equipped to overcome them. So listen to God. Trust Him. His way is always best!

DAY 364

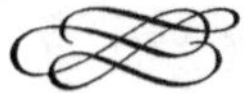

"I'd rather be the shortest player in the majors than the tallest player in the minors." Fred Patek

He tried to get a look at Jesus, but he was too short to see over the crowd. Luke 19:3

Zacchaeus was a short man. We don't know exactly how tall he was but his lack of height prevented him from seeing Jesus over the crowd. So Zacchaeus climbed a tree to see the Son of God. And his efforts didn't go unnoticed. Jesus saw him and insisted on being a guest in his house. Zacchaeus would soon repent for his sins and pledge repayment to those he had cheated. He received salvation that night. His lack of height didn't matter. But his heart did. Zacchaeus was willing to go to great lengths and heights in order to see The Savior, for an encounter with Jesus. Are you willing to do the same today? Are you willing to put your physical limitations aside in order to be in Jesus's presence? The outcome can and will be life changing!

DAY 365

"The doctors x-rayed my head and found nothing." Dizzy Dean

So they went in, but they didn't find the body of the Lord Jesus. Luke 24:3

Normally, being empty is never a good thing. Empty gas tank, empty bank account, empty stomach, never an emptiness you want to experience. But as believers of our Lord and Savior Jesus Christ, the empty tomb is a good thing! The empty tomb is a powerful symbol. It represents hope. It represents triumph. And it represents the assurance of eternal life. Jesus defeated death. He defeated injustice and wrongdoing in our fallen world. And in doing so, the power of darkness no longer has the final word. Neither does guilt, condemnation, shame or loss. Nothing will ever separate you from the love and the power of Christ. And we know this to be true because of the empty tomb. Thanks be to God!